Are You Really OK?

Are You Really OK?

Understanding Britain's Mental Health Emergency

Stacey Dooley

1

BBC Books, an imprint of Ebury Publishing,
20 Vauxhall Bridge Road,
London SW1V 2SA

BBC Books is part of the Penguin Random House group of companies
whose addresses can be found at global.penguinrandomhouse.com

First published by BBC Books in 2022
This paperback edition published in 2023

www.penguin.co.uk

A CIP catalogue record for this book is available from the British Library

ISBN 9781785947032

Printed and bound in Great Britain by Clays Ltd, Elcograf S.p.A.

The authorised representative in the EEA is Penguin Random House Ireland,
Morrison Chambers, 32 Nassau Street, Dublin D02 YH68

To everyone who has ever been affected
by the issues covered in this book.

Contents

Introduction

Over the years, I had hundreds of messages from strangers asking me to make a film about mental health. But for me, there was a temptation to shy away from it, mainly because it's so difficult to get the tone and context right. I mean, there are so many things to take into consideration.

Firstly, can somebody give genuine consent if they aren't always of completely sound mind? This was my main concern when I was talking to my commissioner, executive producer and director about the possibility of filming in a mental health unit in 2019.

I had reservations. The execs and I went over all the possible drawbacks again and again, and we always came back to the conclusion that there was hopefully more to gain than lose: that the benefits outweighed the problems that could occur. Not enough people understand or accept the things that can go wrong with our mental health – and if people don't know what's going on then they can't help others or themselves. There are a lot of misconceptions around it – that people with mental health problems are violent or dangerous, for instance, or they're weird or self-indulgent and could get better if they wanted to. This creates stigma and leads to discrimination, which just makes the situation worse.

When you actually listen to people talk about their mental health problems, you realise that the stereotypes are way off. We all have a rough time at some point in our lives and for some of us poor mental health will be part of that. Whose life is perfect? Who doesn't have hurdles to overcome? Every young person I've met contends with anxiety, pressure and the sense of feeling overwhelmed to a certain extent. Obviously, some people's experiences are way more severe than others but mental health affects us all – and even more so now, in the aftermath of a pandemic.

Still, if we were going to film in a mental health unit, we knew we had to try to do it in the most responsible way possible. We wanted to make sure that our contributors felt safe and secure in the knowledge that we were there for the right reasons. The best way to do that was to give them something called 'rolling consent', which is quite unusual when you're making a film. Typically, the person you're filming will give verbal consent, then you get written consent and you take your footage off to the edit and make the film that you want to make. But with this film we understood that there were deeper complexities. Offering rolling consent meant we would film if the contributors were happy to be filmed but if at any point they wanted to change their mind, they could.

In one case, we had extensive conversations on film with one young woman, with her mother and with the doctors who were treating her – and then she had a change of heart.

'I don't want to be a part of it anymore,' she said, so we took her out of the film.

In a situation like that, of course you're gutted because you think, 'This is so powerful. I want her to stay in the documentary.' But above all else, you have to prioritise the people you're filming and respect their wishes.

It was also important to negotiate the trust of the doctors and healthcare staff who were contributing to the film. I'm so thankful that they took a chance on letting us in. We said, 'We promise we won't take advantage of this situation,' but they couldn't know what would happen when the footage was put together in the edit, after we left the facility and the production team got involved in making the final show. So, credit to the staff for saying, 'Actually, we believe you and we need to get this out there.'

In late 2019, we filmed for several weeks inside a mental health unit at Springfield hospital in south London. It was a real eye-opener for me – a really steep learning curve – and it resulted in a documentary for BBC3 entitled *On the Psych Ward.*

Over the course of making it, I met several youngsters who had been admitted to the unit with serious problems like anxiety, psychosis, depression, anorexia and personality disorder; some of them were at crisis point and had been detained, or 'sectioned', under the Mental Health Act. As they opened up about how hard it is to live with a serious mental health condition, and how devastating the impact on them and their families, I realised that some of them had had moments when it could have gone either way, when they've felt suicidal and overwhelmed, and thought, 'What's the point?' You couldn't fail to see how crucial our mental health services were in helping these youngsters find their way towards recovery.

When you're filming in a situation like this, the biggest fear is that you don't want to say the wrong thing. You don't want to rock the boat, get it wrong, cause distress or be made an example of. But as long as you're really transparent about the fact that you're not claiming, for one second, to be an expert, then I think it's worth doing. This was about us, as ordinary individuals, trying to understand and learn what these people were going through. It was about having frank, candid conversations and saying, 'I don't know where you're coming from. I can't imagine what this feels like but I'm here, I'm listening and I want to make sure that you feel respected and that you're not going to be judged.' Because even when you don't know what it feels like to be in crisis, you can certainly try to learn how to empathise and show compassion.

One of the guys who was admitted to Springfield while we were filming asked me if I had ever suffered from mental health problems. All I can say is that I know what it feels like to have anxiety, although not to the same extent as some of the people I met at Springfield. I can't imagine what it must feel like to be completely overwhelmed by anxiety, to think,

'This is bigger than me.' But there were moments when I was younger, especially when I was in my teens, where I would feel very anxious, apprehensive and frightened – and when you're that young and you're panicking and you feel like you're losing control, it's terrifying. You think you're going to die. 'What the hell is going on?' you think.

The advice often was, 'Take a minute. Breathe in for five, hold for five, out for five.' Sometimes I found that just a simple coping mechanism like that could help and I'd start to think, 'Everything's going to be OK.'

I'm very grateful that anxiety is no longer really an issue for me. I'm lucky because as an adult, although arguably I have much more to be anxious about, I feel very calm, on the whole. Having said that, there have been situations at work where I've felt myself starting to go. When I've been on a tiny plane flying over the north of Nigeria, for instance, or in a chopper, bouncing all over the sky in Mexico. I hate flying anyway but when it's that turbulent I can feel the panic rising up my body and I get a blotchy neck just like when I was younger. 'Get me off this plane!'

Then it's 'In for five, hold for five, out for five …'

Katie, the director of *On the Psych Ward*, already had great relationships with the staff at Springfield because she'd been recceing the hospital for a while. Everyone seemed very down to earth. When we arrived, a really sweet young girl showed us around; we met the lad who did the rounds taking the blood pressures, and the doctors and nurses were friendly and welcoming. The hospital didn't feel like a sanitised, strict environment; it felt very informal and relaxed. We had a cup of tea and started to loosen up and get to know people.

At first, I listened in on the discussions the mental health staff were having about some of the people who had come to the Lotus Assessment Suite, a special unit that offers a calming environment away from A&E if you're experiencing a mental health crisis. Patients can be referred from A&E, a Street Triage team or a Crisis and Home Treatment team, and I think the staff there would describe it as a place to exhale, where people can take a moment to try to digest what's going on, how they're feeling and why they're feeling the way that they are. They're surrounded by people and experts who can try to take some of the weight off their shoulders, help them and point them in the right direction.

I was keen to assure the staff that I was here and I was up for it. But when the phone goes and everyone runs to get it, and a lad comes in and he's screaming, and there are grown men trying to hold him back, it's not comfortable. No part of you enjoys watching people suffer. Your heart is breaking for these people who are sick and confused and suffering delusions. There's anger in their eyes; you can see they're tormented. It's uncomfortable because it doesn't feel familiar, and someone is suffering.

As a filmmaker, you come up against this a lot. You have to film elements to really get the story across, to show the outside world what these people are going through, day in, day out. But you also don't want to be too intrusive. So it's a very fine line. You have to make snap decisions, in 15 or 20 seconds: 'Do we film this or not? Is it right to film this?'

You hope you get it right but there's no way of truly knowing.

Some people will commend the rawness; some people may find it gratuitous. Still, with this film and this topic, I feel proud of what we achieved collectively – me, my team, the healthcare experts and, of course, the individuals themselves.

Initially, I was hesitant about getting involved in the conversations because I didn't feel qualified to justify my thoughts. But when we spoke to the healthcare professionals, they said, 'Of course, we can say what we think is best but in many instances you don't have to have studied what we've studied to be part of the conversation.'

Most of the discussions about people who had been brought into the unit were on the lines of, 'Do we admit them? Do we send them back home?' Years ago, the common approach was to keep people who were unwell in hospital and separate them from the general public, but as we've learnt and evolved, we've realised that it's much more helpful to have them out of the hospital as much as possible and place more of the resources and services in the community.

After a few days, the staff started asking me, 'What do you think? What would you do?' It forced me to think, 'What is right?'

A good example of this was with Kyle, one of the lads who featured in the film. When I met Kyle, he was feeling deeply depressed and suicidal; he came to Lotus because he didn't know how to get out of the depression. 'I've been to A&E with these sorts of problems before but there's only so much they can do because they've got too many people to deal with,' he said.

One of the doctors asked Kyle whether he had any plans to harm himself. Kyle said he didn't but was worried that he might suddenly do something on impulse, as had happened before.

'What would we want admission to achieve?' the doctor said, when we met to discuss whether Kyle should be admitted or not. 'Lotus is here not because we don't want to admit people but because all of the resources are going into the community,' she went on. 'For someone like Kyle, I think we need to try to support him to give all these things a go. Then, if it doesn't work, he's always got a route back where we can think about the plan again.'

I had so much respect for the staff because it was always so tricky. Part of me was thinking, 'Oh no, he's going to harm himself.'

Kyle was sent home and therapy put in place for him. I could see the logic of not admitting him to hospital: the ward is not the real world and it's not what life looks like, and to get better you have to experience reality. But I couldn't help worrying. I don't think I've met anyone who felt as defeated as Kyle in my life and I have been on frontlines in war zones and in refugee camps; I've met survivors of sexual violence and people who have been tortured by drug cartels.

Kyle appeared devoid of emotion, just empty. The first day I filmed him, I met my partner Kev afterwards and we went to our favourite Indian. Everyone in the restaurant seemed on great form, eating out and enjoying time with their families, and I said to Kev, 'I can't stop thinking about this lad; he is just so sad.'

It made me really emotional. I just couldn't imagine what it must be like to feel that empty. Whenever I thought of Kyle after that, I'd think, 'Where is he now? What's his situation?'

Kyle kindly agreed to speak to me for this book and I was able to follow up and find out where he was and how he was coping during lockdown. He was willing to talk about his condition in more depth because he knew how helpful it could be to other people and I was very grateful to him for opening up again.

While we were making the film with Kyle and the other contributors, I could feel how strong the subject was. Then, after it was broadcast, the response was massive – I had hundreds of messages from people saying, 'This has been my life for *x* amount of years! Thank you so much for taking on such a difficult subject.' I heard from people living with mental health conditions and from people who had come through the system and out the other side. And from nurses and doctors working within the sector. I was pleased that we'd had the courage to go ahead.

Then, in February 2020, I did an event at the Barbican in a room packed with nearly 2,000 interested, curious, young people. Towards the end of the evening there was a Q&A and a girl in the crowd put her hand up. In front of all these strangers, she said, 'I was really made up to see the film you made at Springfield hospital because I was a patient in that mental health unit, on that ward. I've come out the other end now and I've put my hand up today because I want people to know that recovery is possible.'

It must have taken a lot of courage for her to speak out and be so candid, and after she'd finished, there was, quite rightly, a massive round of applause – the whole of the Barbican was clapping her – which must have been amazing for her. And so bloody deserved.

I was delighted and remember thinking, 'This is why you make these documentaries, isn't it? For people like this girl, who have lived it and then see it on the telly and think, "Yes, that was a massive chapter in my life but now I'm here: I'm working, I'm in a functioning relationship and I respect myself."'

Positive stories like hers can inspire people going through mental health problems and those around them. Recovery is rarely linear but is absolutely possible – a very strong message, but just hearing it may give you that bit of hope you need to keep going through the tough times. It doesn't necessarily mean you can be completely free of your illness, of course, but that with the right help you can get through a crisis, manage your mental health and carry on living as normally as possible. (Whatever 'normal' is!)

The huge response to *On the Psych Ward* prompted the BBC to commission a follow-up documentary in the same hospital in late 2020. Mental healthcare workers had been saying for months that they were anticipating a 'tsunami' of post-Covid-19 mental health problems in young people, so in the next film we looked at what was happening as a result of the global pandemic.

Making these films got me thinking about how well this subject would lend itself to a book. Using the documentaries as a springboard and working in collaboration with mental health experts and charities to find contributors and help tell their stories responsibly and in-depth, I could shine a light on life on the mental health frontline and give a voice to young people throughout the UK who are living with mental health conditions across the spectrum.

My first book, *On the Frontline with the Women who Fight Back*, focused on women's experiences of extreme and difficult circumstances around the world. I've been fortunate enough to meet many remarkable people over the last decade of making documentaries – sometimes in incredibly hostile environments where they've been really up against it – and I've seen the devastating effect that poverty, trauma, violence, abuse, stigma, stress, prejudice and discrimination can have on people's mental health. It has been the common thread in much of the work I've done.

Mental health issues have also affected the film crews I've worked with, which isn't surprising when your camera people have covered war, death and genocide – the darkest parts of humanity. I once worked on location with a guy who suffered with crippling PTSD. He seemed unreasonable in his responses but it didn't come from a place of malice: he was just very snappy, very agitated, very annoyed about the smallest things. He rocked back and forth a lot and one day I found him on the floor, curled up in a ball. In the course of interviewing people for this book, I've met survivors of domestic abuse who describe having similar symptoms of PTSD.

Another time, I was part of a big crew and we were abroad. One of the crew members was there to keep everyone safe and healthy but she unexpectedly had a psychotic episode and totally unravelled in front of our eyes. Her deterioration was very rapid: she seemed quite healthy and then there were just a few odd behavioural moments; two days later she was talking in riddles to me across the dinner table, holding my hand and telling me 'they' were coming for us. It was surreal.

What do you do in that situation? You don't want someone to know that you're freaked out by what's happening but you also don't want to indulge the delusions. It's a tricky one to get right.

I learnt later that this crew member had a history of mental health problems, even though her psychosis appeared to come out of the blue. I think this is one of the frightening things about mental health – it can appear to change very rapidly and dramatically, as was the case with a young woman I met at the Lotus unit. This young woman seemed very ordinary and relatable. She was informed, fun and beautiful, and a professional with her own flat in London. On the surface, she seemed healthy; she reminded me a lot of my friends. She seemed to have a great relationship with her mum and her mum seemed to truly love her. She never spoke of any trauma or any incident that had scarred her. But she was having psychotic episodes and had lost who she recognised herself to be.

I spent quite a lot of time with this particular person and there were moments where she seemed completely fine, then I would ask a question and she would give an entirely inappropriate response or say something that I was almost certain she didn't believe. Then she'd be like, 'Oh, shit,' and I was suddenly brought back to the fact that she was really unwell. It was very sobering because for the five or six minutes leading up to that moment, we'd just been talking about music or how she'd done her hair. Sometimes, it appeared that she understood what was going on and where she was, and other times when she couldn't quite comprehend it because the world was suddenly very foreign to her.

Her relatives couldn't believe that they were sat in a mental health unit with her. They were saying, 'We can't even begin to articulate what's going on because we don't get it.'

It was frightening because I realised that if it could happen to this young woman then it could happen to anyone. She was partly why, in the course of writing this book, I wanted to find out more about psychosis. I wanted to hear more about what it feels like to experience delusions – and anxiety, depression, anorexia, schizophrenia, addiction, substance abuse, self-harm, PTSD and personality disorders. I also wanted to look at the environmental and social factors that impact or trigger people's mental health issues and ask, how wide is the gender divide and how do race and sexuality intersect with mental health?

In order to open up the conversation about mental health in young people and challenge the stigma and stereotypes around it, I needed to learn more about it by engaging with the people affected by it and hearing their accounts of what they have been through, how they have treated their problems and their recovery or how they are managing them going forward. So I set about interviewing people about their mental health experiences and issues, and also talked to experts about the bigger picture in each area of focus, from gambling addiction to the trauma inflicted by domestic abuse, about the services available, the things that need to change and how we, as a society, can support people affected by these issues.

Mainly, I wanted to put young individuals and their experiences at the centre of the book. We need to listen to them and we need to ask: how can we help as many people as possible to be the best versions of themselves?

The World Health Organization (WHO) states that the most important barrier to overcome in the community is stigma and discrimination towards people with mental health and behavioural disorders. We have to chip away at that stigma so that people feel able and empowered to seek the help they need; otherwise they will avoid telling others about what they are going through and try to mask their symptoms.

The Equality Act 2010 makes it illegal to discriminate against people with mental health problems but that doesn't mean it's not happening. Just because mental health is difficult territory – and it's far easier not to discuss difficult things – doesn't mean we shouldn't explore it. It's worth remembering that if we left important issues solely to those who are directly affected by them then there's a risk nothing would change. You'd only ever have gay people fighting for gay rights or Black people fighting for BLM. That's not what it's about.

True equality is everyone – the majority – standing up and saying, 'Look, we have to talk about this.'

This book is about opening up that conversation.

1

The Experts

Sean

Over the course of making the *On the Psych Ward* films, I met a lot of remarkably inspiring people who work in psychiatry and mental health care. The conversations I had with these people, who were all incredibly knowledgeable and compassionate, made me think that the best way to begin a book about mental health would be by going straight to the experts for an overview of where we are now.

So I approached Sean, a leading consultant psychiatrist at the unit where we filmed, to see if he would be willing to help. Sean has been a psychiatrist for a long time and, as a clinical director at a big NHS mental health trust, is arguably at the top of his game. (Although he is so modest, he will be mortified by this statement. He used to ask me to just call him Sean, instead of Dr Whyte – 'It's too formal otherwise.') But what really strikes me about him is that, while he is a real intellect, he is very human, full of compassion and understanding, and has a lovely way with his young patients. He also has a knack for describing things in layperson's terms, which is very useful if you're not familiar with mental health terminology. Every time I came out of a meeting with him, I had a sense of total clarity. So he seemed to me to be the ideal person to lay the foundations for this book.

Like me, Sean feels we need to normalise talking about mental health, however inexperienced we are. So he was happy to answer my questions, no matter how basic – and I had quite a few. I started by asking him why people's mental health is so poor at the moment. Because you hear it on the news all the time, don't you? We're in a mental health crisis and it's just getting worse, to the point that it sometimes feels really overwhelming. So what the hell are we going to do?

Sean's reply was surprisingly upbeat. 'If you look historically, mental health at the moment in the UK and other Western societies is probably better than it's ever been,' he said.

So that was interesting. He went on to compare mental health to poverty, which he said is perhaps the lowest it's been for many people in most societies in the whole of human history – extreme poverty affects less than 10 per cent of the global population today, when it was around 40 per cent in the late 20th century, and probably well over 90 per cent in the middle ages. Hundreds of years ago, he explained, people began challenging the idea that poverty is a fact of life that we should just accept. Instead it was something that could be changed and should be changed, and that we should look at structuring society differently so that wealth could be more evenly distributed.

The change in attitudes to mental health came a lot more recently but over the past 200 years, people have begun to realise that having behavioural and psychological issues doesn't condemn you to a terrible existence where you feel awful all the time.

'We've stopped saying, "That's just who you are. Tough; live with it,"' Sean said, 'and we've started saying, "These are things that can be changed."'

It's a huge step. We now accept that things can be done to improve mental health – and that we should do these things.

Sean thinks this kind of insight has come from telling stories to each other as a society about our own lives: dramas, soap operas, reality TV shows, documentaries and books all give us the chance to see what an impact different values and ways of doing things have on other people's experiences. His outlook makes things seem more promising than I was expecting. But if we're in a reasonably good place now, why does it feel as if mental health has never been more fragile? I asked him if he thought it was because we're more aware of how much mental ill health and poor mental wellbeing there is out there.

'It feels like a much bigger problem than it did when we all had our heads in the sand,' he agreed. 'But there's still a really long way to go before we've all got good mental health and we routinely don't do things that have a negative impact on ourselves and others.'

Something I've always wondered is if it's the case that all mental health issues can be hereditary – if they can be about your genetics or DNA.

Sean said that if you've got a first degree relative – someone you share 50 per cent of your genes with, such as a parent – with a primary mood disorder like bipolar disorder or recurrent depression, or a first degree relative with schizophrenia, there is an increased risk of getting or developing it yourself. 'But there are much bigger risk factors for mental ill health than genetics – and at the top of the list of risk factors is your experience of being sexually or physically abused or emotionally neglected in childhood,' he said. 'Recurrent substance use is really important too. That's a bigger risk factor for many mental disorders than genes or almost anything apart from childhood abuse.'

Childhood abuse is the risk factor I'm probably most familiar with, given some of the documentaries I've worked on over the last 15 years. Studies show that one in three adult mental health conditions relate directly to adverse childhood experience (ACE) and I've had conversations with some really powerful people while making the *On the Psych Ward* films who've had a hellish time of it during their childhood. When they start describing their experiences as children, you're almost not surprised they're so poorly now because no one was there to look after them when they were tiny.

However, it doesn't necessarily follow that if you've experienced childhood abuse, you will become mentally unwell, Sean told me: 'What's amazing is how high a proportion of people who have awful early experiences are very resilient and go on to be fine mentally,' he said. 'It's something I don't think is really recognised in society. There's a sense that there's cause and effect: you have a terrible experience and therefore you'll go on to be depressed for the whole of your life. But it's not like that at all. The majority of people survive and overcome it.'

It was heartening to hear this. But is anyone exempt? Can a person ever be immune to mental health issues?

No, according to Sean, although it is possible to be insulated from them. So, if you had a privileged upbringing, if you're lucky not to have inherited any genes that predispose you to illness and you were loved as a child, made to feel valued, had a good schooling and you feel you are capable of achieving things – all of this would insulate you from experiencing poor mental wellbeing.

'But if enough wrong things happen that exceed someone's ability to cope, no matter how privileged they are, they will get ill,' he said.

He said that schooling is another key factor in mental health. 'School is where you get a sense of whether you can have an alternative life, whether things about your life are changeable and whether you can grow as a person and learn skills you didn't have before; it's where you have role models such as teachers to look up to and to aspire to become and believe more is possible for you. Your experience of employment is another factor because it's a route to being able to gain social status and earn money to do the things you want.'

I asked him what needs to change fundamentally for us to be in a better position, 10, 20 or 30 years down the line. He seemed hopeful that things would go on improving. 'The fact that we're talking about causes like Black Lives Matter, although the movement is not directly about mental health, is so important for the kinds of social change that will massively benefit people's mental health,' he said.

Certainly, in my conversations with people for this book, it has been eye-opening hearing about the wear and tear of everyday racism that affect the Black community, the stereotypes young adults of colour have grown up with and the templates given to them by teachers. I've also heard about the prejudice affecting LGBTQ+ young people and how coming out to your family, friends and work colleagues can cause an incredible amount of anguish if there's a negative reaction. So it's encouraging that Sean thinks there is a growing sense that it's not OK for any group in society, or any individual, to be disregarded or treated less well than others, and that it's not OK for us to ignore the impact of lesser treatment on people's wellbeing.

He suggested that, although it's vital to fund mental health services and awareness programmes in schools, perhaps social changes are more important, in the long term.

'You're saying that, as long as we're having these conversations about social change and what our society looks like – and we try to make sure everyone's prioritised in a way that they need to be – it will help us to get a grip on the poor mental health that currently exists?'

He nodded. 'I think it will make a massive difference.'

He is of the opinion that along with making structural and social changes, we need a preventative approach to mental health. 'Ideally, we'd have public health interventions that would lead to the problem not occurring in the first place, with people being more resilient and less likely to have those situations occur that can impact mental health negatively,' he said. 'Then, in the long term, you might need to spend less on services like the ones in the NHS, which are about trying to address the problem way after it's already happened.'

Prevention over cure makes so much sense. Sean used a simple analogy. 'A trauma surgeon may patch someone back up and help repair their broken bones after they've had a motorcycle or car accident but really, the road safety measures needed to be there to begin with, along with the laws against drink driving and the seatbelt laws.'

Moving on to mental health treatment and medicine, I wanted to know more about psychiatric drugs because I find it so remarkable how we're able to take pills that help us come back from extreme experiences. While we were filming on the mental health wards, I saw drastic transformations in people within a couple of weeks of them being admitted to the hospital. It was so impressive.

'How do these medications work, in layperson's terms, so that I can understand it?' I asked.

Sean returned to the analogy of the trauma surgeon patching someone up after they've had a motorbike accident.

'Have you ever seen when someone's had a complex fracture of a bone, they can have all these pins and metal rods sticking out of their bones, which are held together by one of those big frames?' he said. 'My psychiatrist colleagues would say this isn't a great analogy but you can sort of think of drugs like that. They're not really treating the underlying problem at all but they are prodding the brain in a particular way to function differently and get into a different state, which can make it easier for talking treatments or changes in your lifestyle or social situation to help you recover.'

Take antidepressants, for example. According to government figures, 17 per cent of the UK population (7.3 million people) take antidepressants, mainly to treat clinical depression.

'What's happening in depression is still really poorly understood at the neurobiological level but there are some patterns of changes that are seen in all the brains of depressed people that you scan,' Sean told me. He went on to describe something called the 'default mode network', a set of interconnecting, interacting areas in the brain involved in reflective and introspective thought and memory, which is known to malfunction in depression and many other mental illnesses. One of the areas that influences that network is a set of nerve cells that use serotonin and noradrenaline – chemicals known as neurotransmitters – to send messages to each other and to other parts of the brain. Although doctors know very little about what's happening when the network malfunctions – and can't do much to change it directly – they do know that some medicines affect the area where the cells are communicating with serotonin and noradrenaline.

Sean explained that the pills work in a variety of different ways: they make the downstream nerve cells more receptive to the message; they cause the upstream cells to increase the volume of the message and they change what are called feedback loops.

'To use another analogy,' he said, 'if I started shouting at you and it came really loud out of your iPhone, you might back off a bit, move away from the phone. Nerve cells do the same thing: they down regulate or up regulate their receptors – they become more or less sensitive, depending on what's going on.

'If the network is malfunctioning and the cells have become down regulated, they're closing their ears to the message "Be happy". Medicine gets those nerve cells to start synthesising new receptor molecules that work better and put them on the membrane of the cell, so that the message can be heard more clearly. And that process of synthesising new proteins is what takes two to three weeks, which is why antidepressants take that long to have their full effect.

'So you're influencing one part of this malfunctioning network and, for reasons we don't understand – we just know that it helps a lot of people – this can kickstart the network to function in a healthier fashion. After a few months of this – and we know that the longer you've been depressed, the longer the treatment needs to be – you can withdraw the drug and the network will carry on functioning normally, in the same way that the bone has healed and you can take the metal rods out again.'

I asked him if you're more likely to respond positively to antidepressants if you take them earlier on – if you have felt depressed for a longer period of time, is it less likely that the medication will work?

'As a rule of thumb, yes,' he said.

So little is understood about depression but I wondered if he knew why some people just don't feel the benefits of antidepressants.

'We know a little bit of that. Hopefully, we're only a couple of years away from being able to genotype people and say, "I predict, from having looked at your genome, that you'll respond to this drug and you won't respond to that one." We can already do this for a drug called clozapine, for instance, which is used for schizophrenia, although the genetic test isn't widely available.'

There are 20,000 or so known genes in the human genome – the complete set of genetic information we all have – and every person's gene set is unique. So decisions about which drug is best for you will, in the future, be made based on your individual genes, receptor subtypes and the enzymes in your liver that break down the drugs and do or don't stop them getting to the brain. It sounds like big changes are coming to psychiatric medicine.

'In a few years' time, hopefully, treatment for depression will be much more targeted, in the way that breast cancer treatment already is,' Sean said.

Another area of mental health that I find really interesting is psychosis. I spent time on a ward with patients experiencing psychosis: some of them were having confused thoughts and seemed 'out of touch' with reality; others were having delusions or hallucinations. It made me think about what was going on in their brains, especially when I saw, in some cases, their mental health improving after treatment.

I asked Sean if the drugs the doctors used to treat patients experiencing psychosis work in a similar or entirely different way to antidepressants?

'In an analogous way,' he said.

He explained that when people experience psychosis, a different network in the brain is malfunctioning, the so-called 'dorsal attention network'. The understanding is that there are several groups of cells that are not working correctly and give rise to the three groups of symptoms that you see in acute psychosis, but exactly how that's happening isn't known.

'One of those groups of cells is made up of neurons that communicate using dopamine,' he said. 'All antipsychotics affect dopaminergic transmission, sometimes on its own, sometimes in combination with a different sort of serotonergic transmission. Again, it seems to be that you somehow prod the network with these drugs that cause one of the malfunctioning groups of cells that are communicating to increase their sensitivity to certain kinds of messages, and that helps the whole network flip into a different state. But that's an incredibly crude and basic explanation of what's going on. We don't really understand how it links to the symptoms – and, interestingly, antipsychotics only treat some of the symptoms.'

While we were filming, I learnt that the symptoms of psychosis are sometimes grouped into 'positive' and 'negative' symptoms. Positive symptoms are changes in thought and behaviour that are 'added on' to a person's experiences, like paranoia, delusions and hearing voices; negative symptoms are changes that 'take away' from their experiences, like apathy, a sense of isolation and loss of sense of self and the power to make choices.

Sean explained that antipsychotic drugs reduce the reality distortion associated with psychosis – one of the two groups of positive symptoms – but they don't touch negative symptoms, and have little impact on the other positive symptom group (conceptual distortion) – and no one is sure why.

'What we do know is that if you treat schizophrenia earlier, you're less likely to develop any negative symptoms in the first place, which is why there's so much less of that around than there was in the wards of the asylums 80 years ago. But if they do develop, not enough is known about what is happening in the brain to treat them effectively.'

Eighty years doesn't seem very long ago. It shows how far we've come.

I asked Sean whether it would be true to say of all mental health issues that the earlier you treat the patient, the more likely they are to respond positively.

He said yes, as a rule of thumb – and not just to medication, for everything. He used family therapy as an example. 'You talk to a family therapist and I'm sure they would say the same thing, that the sooner you can get in with the family before harmful patterns of behaviour become too entrenched, the more likely you are to help the child avoid suffering poor mental health because of the way the whole family is interacting.'

Therapy is another area I'm really interested in. I asked him whether he thought that everyone could benefit from it.

'I'm in favour of therapy and think everyone should have access to it, but it's not the only way to recover,' he said.

What are the other ways?

'Having great teachers at school; being married to or in a relationship with the right person; having a caring friendship group; moving to a new area where society thinks differently. All of these can be just as effective,' he said.

Among my pals and people I really love, there are some who've found therapy tremendously beneficial and they've taken so much from it. You have to find the right therapist, they tell me, but once you've found someone you trust and who you feel is really listening and is on your team, it can be life changing, apparently. Equally, I've had conversations where people have said, 'It's not for me at all. I didn't feel like it was a safe space. And it felt quite self-indulgent. I gained nothing from it.'

I suppose, like with everything in life, you've got to make sure that you've built up a rapport with someone you trust.

Sean agreed that the personal chemistry between the two people in the counselling room is a huge factor in whether it will work. He had therapy as part of his psychiatry training and recommends being assessed by an initial therapist who has access to lots of therapists and can match you with someone suited to help with the issues you come with.

There used to be an assumption that therapy was quite middle class – a bit of a luxury and a bit pricey. If you had money, you didn't have to wait for access to it.

'We know that therapy is available on the NHS but is it the same standard as the therapy you can access privately?' I asked Sean. 'And is there enough therapy within the NHS for people who haven't got disposable income?'

He explained that the NHS has massively expanded the provision of cognitive behavioural therapy (CBT), a form of therapy that there's the most evidence for – and, conveniently, is one of the cheapest to roll out – as part of the Improving Access to Psychological Therapies (IAPT) programme, which provides evidence-based psychological therapies to people with anxiety disorders, depression and other mental illnesses.

'I know that the government gets knocked for a lot of things it gets wrong, but this is one thing, in my view, that it's really, really got right,' he said.

So now you can go to your GP (or call 111, or search online for NHS IAPT) and register for a short course of cognitive behavioural therapy to address anxiety, phobias, depression, OCD, PTSD or just poor mental wellbeing. You'll get maybe six sessions of an hour long of a therapist's time.

'For a huge number of people who don't have a problem big enough to come into secondary care because it hasn't got that bad yet, CBT can stop it in its tracks and enable them to live a much healthier and more fulfilled life,' he said.

It is by no means the answer to everything, he added, but it's still a massive improvement on where we were; it's a good starting point to develop from. He is hoping that other therapies will become more routinely available for people with more complex conditions than depression and anxiety, like borderline personality disorder (BPD), which I saw quite a bit of when we were filming at the hospital. These conditions can be helped with mentalisation-based treatments (MBT) and dialectical behaviour therapy (DBT), which are available on the NHS but can be quite difficult to access unless you've had a series of crises. MBT helps to make sense of our thoughts, beliefs, wishes and feelings and to link these to our actions and behaviours. DBT helps people understand, accept and manage difficult feelings and make positive choices.

'Hopefully,' Sean said, 'in the next few years, we will be able to resource providing these therapies in primary care for the people who will benefit, rather than having to wait until you are having multiple crises.'

I had another question to ask about therapy: is it only necessary when you're in the thick of mental health problems or does it also lend itself as maintenance? Should you continue with therapy once you're feeling well again?

Sean said that there's no one-size-fits-all answer but it could be helpful to think of things in phases: psychological support in a crisis, followed by a treatment phase that's best conducted after the crisis is settled down.

'If you're acutely suicidal, for example, and you're homeless and your partner's dumped you and your benefits have been stopped, now is a terrible time to make you explore the way your father used to make you feel when he hit you because you need to deal with the practical issues first. But once the crisis is over and things are a bit more stable in your life, then that might be a good time to begin exploring the impact of that abuse on your life to help you to think differently about it in a way that enables you to stop being impacted by it so much.'

He spoke about the risk of dependence on therapy, something he had experienced when the time came to end his own group therapy sessions. 'I remember thinking, "But I really enjoy this! I really enjoy being able to chew over all my problems twice a week with you guys and feel understood and valued and listened to. How will I cope without that?" But if I was still doing that now, 15 years later, I wouldn't have believed that I could cope with these things by myself, which it turns out I could, and I'd be taking that resource from someone else who needed it more by then.'

He recommended refresher sessions of therapy as and when needed, rather than maintenance.

What he said reminded me of a women's prison in America where I filmed. There's a ward with the lifers and a ward with the girls who are only there for, say, 10 or 15 years, and the staff treat them in a totally different way. They don't want the girls with shorter sentences to become institutionalised because there's a risk they'll then feel like they can't cope on their own in the outside world. So they push them harder than they push the lifers, maybe, so that they don't feel too well looked after. 'By the end of it, we don't want them to panic and think, "Oh, I can't leave. I can't do this!"' the warders told me.

Sean reminded me of when, during my early days filming at the Lotus Assessment Suite, I talked to the doctors about how it seemed harsh that they were pushing people to go back home after 48 hours, even when they said, 'I don't feel ready.'

'The time scale is different but it was exactly the same thing,' he said. 'There was a real risk that if we admitted them and they had a couple of weeks in hospital, it would then be even harder to go back to the stresses of life in the outside world.'

'I remember it well,' I said, 'because it felt really strange to me, as an outsider. I wrongly assumed that if someone is unwell, they need to be kept in hospital but actually the vast majority of the services are within the community. We don't want to be keeping people in hospital in the way that we used to.'

I was very grateful to Sean for being so generous with his time and so patient in giving me answers. My final question to him was, 'What would you say to those who have suffered with mental health or are currently suffering?'

He didn't hesitate. 'I'd say, have hope. For everyone, no matter how awful the situation you are in, no matter how bad the mental illness or the mental disorder is, it can improve. Yes, there are conditions that have a worse prognosis than others but everything can improve. At the very least, help can stop things getting worse. For everyone, it can make it at least a little bit better, a little bit less hard to deal with. And for the vast majority of people, it can make it a whole amount better and for a very big proportion of people, it can get rid of the problem entirely, with the right sort of help from people around you – including health services but not just health services.

'You're still just as valuable a person, despite what you're going through. You may want to shut yourself away and fear judgement from other people and worry that people are going to stare at you because you feel odd in one way or another, but you are still just as valuable a person and you deserve just as much care and attention as everyone else, if not more at the moment because of what you're going through.'

It was so great to hear this from an expert, who was speaking from experience because he's seen it so often. The majority will become well. Recovery is entirely possible. It's not always linear but it is possible.

2

Depression

Kyle

When I first met Kyle, he was deeply depressed. He'd come to the Lotus Assessment Suite at Springfield University Hospital in south London because he was in crisis and worried that he might make an attempt at suicide.

Kyle wasn't planning to do anything to himself. 'But a lot of my bad thoughts are really impulsive and intrusive, so I can be laying on my bed and they just come into my head,' he explained. 'They feel like normal thoughts but they're not my thoughts, really – they just appear.'

If you're really suffering, like Kyle was, you can go to the Lotus Assessment Suite for support and stay for up to two days without having to be admitted onto a ward or detained under the Mental Health Act. The aim of the staff there is to contain the crisis and any thoughts about self-harm and suicide before someone goes home.

'If you're in Springfield, you can't act on your bad thoughts and that was one of the main reasons I wanted to go there: it was the safest place to be,' Kyle said.

Kyle and I met in 2019 while we were filming *On the Psych Ward*. The staff I came across at Springfield were brilliant: they knew exactly what we were trying to document and often came to us with potential contributors. When the team and I heard about Kyle, I introduced myself and had a conversation with his mother first and then with his father. When you meet people in this sort of situation, you spend quite a long time with the camera switched off on the floor, building up a rapport with them and making sure they understand what the documentary is about and the reason we're doing it. We made it clear to Kyle and his parents that if they agreed to take part, they had rolling consent and could pull out at any time.

'Let's do this and see if you feel comfy and if it works for your family,' we said.

'Rolling consent' was paramount and we couldn't have made the documentary without it, because quite rightly there were concerns. How can someone give true consent if they aren't always of sound mind, if they're having an episode of psychosis or feel very anxious or depressed, when their judgement could be clouded? We have a duty of care towards people who allow themselves to be filmed, so our relationships with contributors will go on for weeks and months – years, even –

because things evolve and people change their minds. It's not like we turn up, shoot and then say, 'Bye!'

Kyle allowed us to film him in the hope that telling his story would help other people. We built up a great working relationship with him and his folks – Kyle is very sweet and his family were really lovely. That's what breaks your heart: you meet him and you're floored by how low he is and you immediately fall for him because you don't want to see anyone feeling like that. Then you meet his folks and see that they're just regular people trying to look after their family and prioritise the kids. Kyle is not the only unwell person in his family, so his parents have a lot to deal with.

I spoke to his dad about the stress of living with someone who is so on the edge. He replied that he was always checking the bathroom at intervals during the night for signs that Kyle had self-harmed. 'You wake up every morning dreading going in there because you don't know what you're going to find,' he said.

Still, he was trying to stay positive: 'The fact that he's still talking and asking for help gives me hope.'

People often start to feel a bit brighter at Lotus because they feel safer there – and just having that breathing space if they're feeling overwhelmed can help them carry on living their lives. But as 48 hours is the maximum length of time anyone can stay, some individuals may well leave the unit in a similar headspace to the one they were in when they arrived.

Kyle was still very flat as he left the unit. 'I feel so empty,' he told me.

I really felt for him and worried that he might be a danger to himself at home. The staff at Springfield were also very concerned.

'I would say the hardest part of the job is making the decisions about people's care and knowing whether you're doing the right thing, because you can never be 100 per cent certain,' one of the professionals said, admitting that she sometimes got home from work feeling upset by a decision she'd been faced with.

Thirteen days later, Kyle was back at Springfield, after another bout of self-harm. This time he was admitted onto a ward for two weeks.

My team and I were apprehensive when *On the Psych Ward* came out because mental health is such difficult territory to try and cover, for obvious reasons. How would people react? Still, we felt in our hearts that we had tried to work as ethically as possible. Morally we felt comfortable; people who didn't want to be included were cut out of the film and, by the time we broadcast, the remaining contributors knew they were going to be included – their families knew, we'd spoken to the healthcare professionals and everyone felt as comfortable as possible. When appropriate, we show people their contribution as it will appear in the documentary before the show goes out, so there are no surprises and they aren't left to worry or speculate.

Then the film aired and everyone wanted to know, 'How's Kyle doing? What's his situation now?' He struck a chord with so many people.

I thought a lot about him in the year after we'd made *On the Psych Ward*, so I was really pleased to be able to catch up with him online for the book, about a year after I'd last seen him. Kyle is such a lovely, kind soul – really curious and eloquent. It seems to me that he has so much to offer and to give.

I asked how he was.

'I'm OK,' he said. 'Up and down. Better than the last time we spoke.'

How had he felt when he watched the documentary?

'Yeah, I watched the whole thing and it was good.'

I was so pleased that he liked it. I told him about the great feedback we'd had about the film and especially how courageous everyone thought he and the others had been to speak so honestly about what they were going through. I'm aware that some people think there's no place for cameras in a mental health hospital but I honestly believe it can be extraordinarily helpful – so long as it's documented in a sensitive way where you respect everyone involved. If we're going to try to chip away at the stigma around mental health, we have to show it through an honest lens: we have to show that the highs can be high and the lows are low. (And sometimes terrifying.) So when contributors like Kyle say they are happy with what we showed on screen and, in Kyle's case, hope it helps people, I try not to care what some journalists, who have been fortunate enough to not have these experiences, write.

It's undeniable that the documentary – and Kyle's involvement in it – helped people. So many of them wrote and tweeted about Kyle's story, so I was looking forward to hearing what had happened to him since we'd last met.

A year on, he seemed so much better to me than he had before – quite well, even. He looked good physically and I was surprised at how talkative he was and how willing to engage in conversation. But what did I know?

Firstly, I wanted to find out if it had helped him to spend that initial 48 hours at the Lotus Assessment Suite. How had he felt when he went back home that first time?

'I felt like really nothing had changed – and nothing changed for a while,' he told me.

What happened on his return to Springfield, 13 days later? Was he detained?

'I wasn't sectioned. They said I should probably go to the ward and I agreed,' he said.

If you are feeling mentally unwell and considered to be a risk to yourself or to other people, you may be sectioned under the Mental Health Act 1983 and kept in hospital for some time, depending on which section of the Act you are detained under. But you can also be admitted as an 'informal patient', which means your rights are less restricted and you have more freedom. For instance, you are allowed visitors and access to the internet, and you can refuse to take medication. You also have the right to leave if you don't want to stay but if your doctor is worried about you harming yourself or others, they may keep you on the ward for anything up to 72 hours while they decide whether you should be sectioned or not.

I asked Kyle about his experience of being on the ward.

'Everyone had their own rooms, which I didn't expect. I thought it would be like a hospital ward,' he said. 'Breakfast was at nine but at that time I wasn't eating, so I didn't wake up for breakfast. I pretty much sat around in there. Visitors weren't allowed in your room, so you had to see them in a visitation room. Otherwise, there's not much to do. They wouldn't let you have phone chargers, so you had to give them your phone to charge.'

I remembered how the staff at Springfield kept back people's chargers because they were worried about the cables being a danger to people who were feeling unstable.

'Sometimes a doctor would come and talk to you but that was it, really,' Kyle went on. 'It was pretty boring. If you sat in your room for too long, someone would tell you to come and sit in the room with the TV. There were a lot of people who'd been there for a few months and I think they were happy to see new people, so a few of them came and talked to me, but I didn't really seek out people to talk to.'

I asked whether it was a comfort or a hindrance to be around people who were also poorly.

'Maybe it would have been different if they had been going through a similar thing,' he said, 'but there weren't many people with my issues there, who I could relate to. It was an acute ward, for people who aren't dangerous but need to be on a ward, so a lot of them were schizophrenics and people with those sorts of problems.'

While Kyle was on the ward, he tried an antipsychotic drug called quetiapine to calm his impulsive thoughts. Often used to treat schizophrenia, quetiapine is supposed to rebalance dopamine and serotonin to improve thinking, mood and behaviour.

'But I built a tolerance to it – and the more you take it the worse the side effects get, so I stopped taking it,' he said.

When I asked if he felt better now, he said, 'I'm not as flat as I was but I don't feel I've really made that much progress. It's been pretty uneventful, just the same old. The problems I had back then are still there.'

'Are you still feeling suicidal?' I asked. 'When we met, you said, "Stacey, I don't see the point."'

'The suicidal thoughts are still there. It goes in a cycle. I'll have periods of time when it's a lot more intense and I'll feel worse, and then it'll be OK for a few days.'

I was curious about whether these thoughts felt totally random or if there were things that triggered them. 'What do those thoughts sound like?' I asked.

'I spiral a lot, so that might be one of the triggers,' Kyle said. 'One thing can go wrong and it's zero to a hundred. Say I stubbed my toe or had an argument with someone – straight away, I'll start thinking, "I should just kill myself. It's not worth it." It's really rapid. Sometimes it can happen quite a lot and other times it's not as bad – it feels like a normal thought but afterwards you think, "I didn't think that. It was something that was in my head."'

It was a clear description of how Kyle's brain can catastrophise even the smallest snag or incident, which must be exhausting for him if he's sometimes doing it on a daily basis.

According to NHS figures quoted by the Young Minds mental health charity, half of all mental health problems manifest by the age of 14, with 75 per cent by age 24. I remembered Kyle telling me that his problems have been going on for years, since way back when he was in primary school, so I asked him to give me a timeline of when they began and how he felt back then.

'I started getting really bad anxiety when I was in Year 5 and Year 6 and couldn't really go to school as much, and then when I went to high school it got really bad and that's when the depression started.'

He could trace the start of his problems back to when he was 10 and 11. When you're that young, I thought, it must be difficult to try and understand what those feelings even are.

'I'd notice that I had physical symptoms,' he said. 'I'd feel really sick and have butterflies really badly. I didn't really understand why it was happening and thought I was sick, but then it stayed for months.'

He was referred to the Child and Adolescent Mental Heath Service (CAMHS). 'I had CBT therapy when I was 11 or 12, which helped, and I started to understand it a bit more.'

I wondered how he had reacted when the experts said, 'We think this is anxiety.' How do you compute that, as a kid? 'Did you understand it?' I asked.

'I kind of understood because my siblings had it to a degree,' he said. His sister had been diagnosed with autism when she was eight and experienced anxiety as part of her condition.

'Can it be a relief at that young age when you're diagnosed because at least you know what it is, or is it frightening?' I asked.

'I don't think it helped being told what it was because it didn't stop it.'

In Year 8, Kyle was referred to the Sutton Tuition and Reintegration Service (STARS), a pupil referral unit for children who are unable to attend school for medical reasons, including mental health. 'When I went to secondary school initially, there were hundreds of people everywhere and I was struggling really badly. Kids are dickheads when they're that young, so it was hard. When I went to STARS, it was much more relaxed and there were only five people in a class. Everyone else there had similar issues and the staff knew how to deal with it a lot better and there was no judgement.'

That must be a key factor in recovery, I imagine, because when you're poorly anyway, if you feel like people are judging you as well, it's another level of angst you don't need.

'My anxiety got better because it was an easier environment to be in,' Kyle agreed.

The latest government figures, which are for 2018/19, show that there were 438,265 temporary exclusions from schools in the UK and 7,894 permanent exclusions. The most common reason for exclusion listed in both categories is 'permanent disruptive behaviour' – bullying and abuse are also listed, but mental health is not specifically mentioned. Eighty thousand of those temporary exclusions are categorised as being for 'other' reasons.

The aim of reintegration schools is to help children get back into mainstream education but Kyle finished his secondary school education at STARS. Afterwards, he went to college and did an electrical course for a year.

'My depression and anxiety came back a bit but was manageable,' he recalled. 'Then, when I did my apprenticeship in the second year, at first it was OK but over time, the anxiety came back really badly and that's when the suicidal thoughts started coming in. I couldn't cope and I quit doing it. I'm not really sure what caused it but I think it was partly being on a building site, in a working environment that was really stressful – there are some weird people on building sites. In 2017 it got really bad again and from that point it's got worse and worse.'

Thinking about what Sean, the consultant psychiatrist at Springfield hospital, had told me about antidepressants and how they can help to balance neurotransmitters like serotonin and noradrenaline in the brain, I asked Kyle if he had tried taking this type of medication.

'I've tried eight or nine different antidepressants over the last few years and none of them have done anything. They've just made me really ill from the side effects,' he said.

'Is there different medication for anxiety and for depression?' I asked because he clearly knew more about these things than I did.

'To a degree,' he said. 'Most of them are the same medication. There are a few antidepressants that are normally prescribed if you also have anxiety – and it deals with both of them – but I'd say that my anxiety shows in different ways now. It's more social anxiety rather than feeling physical things like butterflies or feeling sick. None of the meds have helped with any of it, really.'

Kyle's anxiety about social situations means that he stays in a lot. 'I go to the shops sometimes or my dad tries to help me go out, just for a meal, but I don't like doing it,' he told me. 'I really don't like it when he just turns up at my door and says, "We're going out" because it catches me off guard. Normally the only time I can really go out is if he says the day before, "OK, let's go for breakfast." I'm not sure why. I guess I need mental preparation. I just need to know in advance that I'm going to do something.'

He said that, during lockdown, if anything it had been a relief not to feel pressure to go out or do anything. It gave him an excuse to sit at home, 'which I guess is a good and a bad thing. I isolate myself quite a lot; I still talk to my mates on the phone sometimes but I don't want to go out.'

When antidepressants didn't help, Kyle was smoking weed but after a time he felt mentally slower and experienced paranoia. 'Initially, it feels like it's helping,' he said, 'but I realised it was doing more harm than good.'

This reminded me of a pal I had who used to drink a lot, who'd said that the immediate comfort was good but the next day, he'd think, 'Oh no, why have I done that?' because it just exaggerated everything. It's self-medication, isn't it? So many people do it when they're having a hard time.

'What used to happen was I'd really set myself off – be really suicidal – and then I'd go out and smoke and completely forget all of it,' Kyle said. 'I'd be looking at my phone doing something completely different and just forget everything that had happened. I found it really useful but it's not a sustainable coping mechanism. I tried a few other drugs but it's the same problem so I stopped doing drugs.'

'Have you knocked weed on the head, then?' I asked.

'I haven't smoked for about six months,' he said.

'That's amazing! Well done, mate!'

He looked pleased. 'I seem to be able to do that, just quit things. I'm not quite sure how.'

If only he could pinpoint it, we joked, he could make a fortune. But if medication – and self-medicating – hasn't helped, has he tried therapy like CBT again?

'CBT helped when I was really young but when I had it again in 2017 it didn't help at all,' he said.

Are there other possibilities to explore?

'Recently I had an autism test,' he said. 'I talked to some guy for a few hours and, at the end, he said that he sees traits of autism, but he thinks I have borderline personality disorder (BPD). I didn't see that coming but I've looked into it and it makes sense because it's quite normal for people with BPD to have intrusive thoughts and mood swings and be really impulsive. Hopefully, if that is what I have, I can get therapy for it.'

Kyle hadn't had a confirmed diagnosis for BPD, he said, because it can take years. But wouldn't it be amazing if he could put his finger on what his condition was and hatch a plan to head in the right direction? It shows that it's really worth pushing yourself to explore the different possibilities so that you can try to identify the right treatment.

I wondered if he had a plan going forward.

'Although things are better, at the same time they haven't really changed,' he said. 'I'm really not doing anything. Every day is the same. I just stay at home, really. I'm struggling to think forward because I'm kind of stuck in a cycle.'

He was feeling let down by the mental health teams he'd been in contact with. 'They just pass you around to each other and then say, "Go back to your GP", and it starts again,' he said. 'I stopped trying with them because they're not helping me. I'm also stuck in not having any motivation to do anything. It's sad to say but I have this mindset where I feel like I'm going to be dead soon. I'm always having thoughts like that and don't feel like doing anything because of them.'

If he was thinking these thoughts, I could see why he'd also think, 'So what's the point in planning?'

'How often do those thoughts enter your mind?' I asked.

'A few times every day, sometimes more, sometimes less. It's quite frequent.'

'Does it feel like a real thought, or a thought that's passing through your mind but isn't yours?'

'Weirdly, I think it's a bit of both,' he said. 'I can't really say that it's fully an intrusive thought because I feel like it's true logically, but I also feel it's something that appears in my head.'

Kyle is 20. Of course, we're all going to die at some point, but, based on average life expectancy, he's got nearly 60 years of his life left to live. Only, he doesn't see things from that point of view.

'I don't think of it in a lifespan way. I look at the last few years and how things are now and it's a miracle that I'm even alive,' he said. 'When I think of the probability of some of the things that have happened – past attempts and stuff – the way I'm thinking is the logical conclusion. I know it's morbid to say it, but …'

He was being honest – it was his opinion based on his experiences and what he's been through in the last few years. Try to put yourself in his shoes: if you had those thoughts, numerous times throughout the day, you probably would think, 'What's it all for? What's the point?'

'I don't see a way forward,' he said. 'These problems aren't just going to disappear. They are very constant.'

'Does any part of you allow yourself to feel optimistic?' I asked him. 'In my opinion as somebody who knows little, you do seem a bit better. That suggests recovery – it's never straightforward but it could be possible? And when you hear of other people who have been in similar situations coming out the other end, do you allow yourself to feel excited about that?'

Admittedly, I am an eternal optimist, plus it's easy for me to say because I've never been in Kyle's situation, but I have met people who have come out the other end. When you see them well and functioning and feeling happiness – or just feeling any emotion – you realise you'd be devastated if somebody didn't make it far enough to get to that point. With Kyle, I could so clearly see all of his potential. He has his entire life ahead of him but he didn't see any of that. At least, not right now.

'I've not been optimistic for a good few years, really,' he admitted. 'Maybe I look more alive because of how flat I was before but I don't feel like anything has really changed. I guess back then was a more extreme version of now but I feel like it's very possible it could happen again at any time. I don't know if that's going to happen or if it's just going to stay like this – an up and down cycle.'

Kyle's had such a difficult time of it that his downbeat attitude isn't surprising. But he told me there was more to it than clinical depression.

'My view on the world and everything else is very pessimistic, so that doesn't really help,' he said. 'I'm not sure if I have my viewpoint purely because of how I feel and the things I've been through but I've had a lot of existential problems in the past few years. I'm stuck in the logic of nihilism, which is a philosophical view that there's no meaning to life. Since we're only human and no one can disprove it, and because I think of things really logically and can't really do anything about that, it's one of the main problems for me. It feels really black and white.

'It's an autistic trait, I think, to have a view like that and not to be able to change your mind on it. Something I read recently suggests it could be a signal to BPD because people with BPD see things in a very black-and-white way, so there's no middle ground for them with things like this. A lot of people recognise that it's probably true – that there isn't a meaning to life – and they find positive ways to spin it, which is called optimistic nihilism, but I'm more pessimistic.'

I clearly don't know a huge amount about nihilism but I understand that Kyle, being so bright, is someone who thinks about the bigger picture. His issues are not just about what's happening internally, and his concerns, struggles and stresses, he is also focused on the wider world, as he sees it and knows it.

'I feel that humans and our whole society are really pointless and meaningless; even the idea of meaning is a human concept. And everyone's living in bubbles,' he said. 'I feel like I'm being forced to live my life – and I should be able to not do that, if I don't want to.'

For someone like me, who doesn't lose time to those enormous thoughts, of course it's easier to feel happy and optimistic. 'Ignorance is bliss,' as they say. But if you start thinking about things from an entirely different perspective, I suspect it can be really heavy.

'I have a lot of intrusive thoughts about it and it's always in my mind, so it gets really overwhelming,' Kyle said.

I wonder if those thoughts will feel familiar to a lot of people. 'What's it all about?' 'What's the point?' 'Why are we here?' These are questions that lots of us ask ourselves when we're becoming an adult and we're trying to figure it all out.

'I used to think a lot about the future of humanity and what we're going to do – and then I started thinking that we're going towards nothing,' Kyle said.

He stopped seeing any point in the human cycle of being born, having children and dying, and I can see the sense in that logic. The thoughts he was describing seemed perfectly valid. 'That's the scary part of it,' he said. 'I'd rather someone just said to me, "No, you're crazy." Instead I feel that what I'm saying is very logical and, because of that, no one can tell me I'm wrong, and that makes me feel worse.'

I could relate to some of what Kyle was saying. Over the last 14 years, I have travelled extensively and met the most horrendous characters in the most harrowing circumstances and seen the most depressing situations you can imagine. So people always say to me, 'How are you so optimistic? You've watched children die. You have seen war, smelt death and met paedophiles and cannibals. Why aren't you a complete cynic?'

This is going to sound really cheesy, but I mean it from the bottom of my heart: when you witness all of that – and I have seen the darkest parts of humanity, truly – of course there are moments when you despair and wonder what it's all about. But I hang on to the fact that I have met more decent, good characters than bad in those situations, and that there are so many people trying to cancel what those horrendous figures have done. And I find that you are so amazed by those beautiful, charismatic, funny, principled individuals that you realise, fundamentally, that life is about love and all of the incredible emotions that you can feel as a living being. So there is room for hope and, although it's admirable that he is so honest, in an ideal world (I know, I know), Kyle won't always feel this way and will be able to see things through a different lens.

Kyle is a young lad who has the privilege of living in Britain and has a home and people who love him. But mental health isn't logical – that's not how it works. Surveys show that each year around one in four people in the UK aged 16 and older will experience a mental health problem, and that young people between 16 and 29 are the group most likely to experience depression.

I'm full of gratitude that, so far at least, I've never suffered with depression or suicidal thoughts because I can't even imagine how you get out of bed. That's why I'm so in awe of people like Kyle, who are still putting one foot in front of the other despite what they're going through.

On the day we met online, Kyle's GP got in touch to say that he had received the report on his autism assessment. As a result, Kyle was hoping to be able to access psychodynamic therapy, which could potentially help with the diagnostic process and improve how he was feeling.

'Is that promising?' I asked. 'Do you allow yourself to think, "Right, we're getting there."'

To him, it wasn't that simple. 'I think it's really scary if it is BPD because I've read that a lot of people take ten years to recover from it or find a way to live with it, so in a way I'm hoping it isn't,' he said. 'But from what I've seen of BPD, it describes everything I'm going through to a tee.'

He explained that, as he understood it, the main ways to treat BPD are: the antipsychotic drug quetiapine, which helps with intrusive thoughts; psychodynamic therapy, which focuses on the psychological roots of emotional suffering, and dialectical behaviour therapy (DBT), another type of talking therapy, which is based on cognitive behavioural therapy (CBT) and specially adapted for people who feel emotions very intensely.

'DBT helps you to recognise which of your thoughts are intrusive and find ways to cope with it but it's a really long process,' Kyle said.

He wasn't sure when it would start or how often it would be. 'I've not really reacted well to therapy, except when I was really young, but I'm hoping it's different this time because it's more targeted towards BPD, if I do have that,' he said.

On the one hand, he thought he'd rather not have BPD, while on the other he wanted to be diagnosed so that he could get on and try to treat it. As for therapy, he was also ambivalent. 'The main thing for me is the existential stuff and a therapist isn't going to be able to change any of that,' he said. 'But it's worth a try, I suppose.'

He was back and forth: sometimes he felt he wanted the help and was willing to try anything but he was also asking these massive questions and thinking, 'Really, what's the point?'

I asked him if he found talking cathartic. 'I find it useful but even if it doesn't help, there's no downsides to it. I think it's good to talk about mental health and what you're doing is really important, so I wanted to help if I could.'

Was he still self-harming?

'It's not as frequent anymore but it happens every now and then,' he said.

I was really pleased to hear it was happening less. 'You've got to celebrate the small victories, haven't you?'

He smiled.

When I first met Kyle, he gave me one- or two-word answers and I've never met anybody who seemed as sad as him, no matter what they'd been through. A year later, he appeared to be an entirely different man – much more talkative and charming. I'd certainly never had a conversation that lengthy with him before. Although I'm not an expert (I promise I'll stop with these disclaimers soon!) but rather an outsider looking at something from a distance, I personally feel as though he has made real progress. But, as with other illnesses, he has good days and bad days.

I feel hopeful when I think about Kyle because he is still here, despite having had so many moments when he could have taken his own life. I'm speculating but I feel like there is still fight in Kyle to live.

I'm reminded of something his dad said about Kyle when I first met them at the hospital: 'You can say – and truly believe when you're saying it – that there are times when you don't want to be here and you feel like you want to end it all. But you are still here and you're still talking about this and going to see your GP. There must be a part of you that wants to stick around.'

3

Eating Disorders

Laura, Jess and James

When I first met Laura, she told me she hadn't eaten for two weeks and three days. 'So I'm not really thinking straight,' she said.

Laura was a sweet, lovely girl in her mid-twenties who seemed amazingly articulate, considering what she was going through. She'd been brought to Springfield hospital after making an attempt on her life. 'I couldn't sleep last night and my heart was pounding,' she told me. 'I just didn't want to be alive anymore and I went to a bridge and that's when the police put me on a 136.'

Section 136 of the Mental Health Act means that the police have the power to take you to a place of safety or keep you safely somewhere if they think you have a mental illness and need 'care and control'.

Two days earlier, Laura had been discharged from hospital after a stay of ten days. 'They discharged me because they couldn't deal with my eating disorder,' she explained. 'I feel like I want to die because I hate my body and everything, so I just don't really know what to do.'

This hadn't been her first attempt. 'I do feel like not living would be better than living with anorexia,' she said, later on. 'It's like living with this big monster who makes you feel just so low and just so disgusting. You just then become really self critical. It's like torture every single day.'

Laura said that she probably hadn't had a healthy relationship with food since she was a child. She'd had her first contact with social services when she was 11 and been sectioned at 16, after a period of not eating and self-harming, and thought that her mental health was linked to past traumas, including sexual assault.

It was both alarming and heartbreaking to hear how she felt about her body. 'I just feel like it's really fat and disgusting and it's too much, like I take up too much space,' she said.

In that moment she seemed so small and vulnerable that it was hard to know how to respond. 'Do you think I take up too much space?' I asked.

She smiled hesitantly. 'You're smaller than me anyway, so I wouldn't think that.'

She added that she wouldn't judge someone who struggled with overeating because there would always be a reason behind their behaviour. So she gave herself a really hard time but didn't judge others.

'Why can't you be that kind to yourself?' I asked.

'Because I know I don't deserve it,' she said.

It was tempting to try and rationalise with Laura and say, 'Look, you're beautiful and you have so much to offer. You deserve to be happy.' But the underlying causes of eating disorders can be incredibly complex and when someone is unwell and the illness has clouded reality, it's very difficult to have those conversations because starvation doesn't just affect the body – it also stops the brain functioning normally. Studies have shown that malnutrition makes it more difficult to concentrate, make decisions and stay balanced, and it can bring on depression and anxiety. In fact, although Laura seemed physically and mentally fragile, I was very impressed by how eloquent she was when speaking about her illness.

I asked her if there were times when she felt good.

'When I'm dancing that makes me feel good and I forget about things for a little while,' she said. 'I love dance and it just makes me feel free. When I'm dancing I'm not really thinking of anything else and I'm not really worrying about how I look. When I'm feeling really low and depressed and I feel like a failure, it just helps me feel that maybe I'm not.'

She felt let down by the services she'd come into contact with. 'I have been in and out of relapse this whole year and I think I've not had the right help. With adult services, things have to get a lot worse before they decide to help you.

And then, by the time things get worse, you don't actually want the help.'

Beat, the UK eating disorder charity, estimates that around 1.25 million people in the UK struggle with eating disorders (EDs). Around 75 per cent of them are female and 25 per cent male. A report published by the Health and Social Care Information Centre eight years ago found that the number of hospital admissions for people with EDs has been increasing yearly by around 7 per cent. Referrals to NHS eating disorder services almost doubled in the wake of the Covid pandemic.

When I caught up with Laura again on a video call in September 2020, she was back in hospital, unfortunately. Yet she was as impressive and articulate as ever as she updated me on what had been happening since we'd last met.

'During Covid I struggled a lot,' she said. 'I wasn't able to keep myself safe and struggled with not being able to see loved ones; I struggled with not being able to access the psychology during the pandemic and not being able to do my dance classes, which was my main motivation. I felt alone with my racing thoughts about my body and overwhelming emotions. I didn't want to be alive anymore.

'I now have a new diagnosis of EUPD [emotionally unstable personality disorder] alongside my eating disorder and after several admissions to my local acute psych ward, it was decided that I should go to the personality disorder unit, where they can help me work on both of my diagnoses. Since

May, I have been accessing DBT [dialectical behavioural therapy], group and individual, plus input from the dietician to work on my eating disorder. I'm now in a much more stable place since I first got here. The programme is intense and extremely restrictive and strict, but I'm slowly getting there.'

I was really pleased that she was in a good place and seemed hopeful of being on the right track now. I wondered what was keeping her going.

'I feel like I'm under so much pressure to get this right and for my recovery to be perfect, but I'm trying to take it day by day. It's really consuming to be in my body and to try and accept that that's OK. I have constant thoughts and emotions rushing through my head. I guess I would say that now is probably where I'm doing well and recovering. As long as I follow my meal plan, I can dance, so that's my biggest motivator, plus being able to eventually get out of hospital and see my family. I feel like I'm getting the right help and in fact there's a lot going on beneath an eating disorder besides weight and food. I feel like accessing this therapy programme can get me on the right track forward and to gain the right skills to stay safe in the community.'

Again, she was so descriptive when she talked about her illness. 'It feels like an overwhelming bubble of emotions around body image,' she went on. 'Every little bite is incredibly hard, constantly thinking about food and weight; there's never a break.'

It sounded exhausting, like it never lets up. 'No matter what weight I am, I still struggle immensely and nothing is ever good enough,' she said, adding, 'Eating disorders come in all shapes and sizes.'

I felt there were definitely reasons to be hopeful after our catch up. And what a bloody superstar Laura was to agree to speak to me again, especially as she was still poorly.

'It's important to know that having an eating disorder at any weight is serious and can cause lifelong damage,' she told me. 'If a young person asked me for advice, I would highlight just how much this struggle is valid, no matter what, and you deserve and need the help. Talk to a teacher, your GP, your family, because you're worth the help. The earlier you intervene the better.'

These are words that resonate with Jess, a trained psychotherapist who has lived experience of EDs and also works for the eating disorder charity Beat in various capacities, including training, website writing and media liaison. I approached her because I thought she might be able to shed more light on what Laura and people like her might be going through.

Everybody's story is different but it was interesting to hear what Jess had to say because she has struggled with EDs, come out the other side and gone on to study them from a clinical point of view. She seems like the ideal person to reach out and help others – I imagine that if you're unwell and you see someone stood in front of you who's been through something similar and is now so well, it must make you feel quite hopeful – and trusting.

'Quite often, what I'm asking them to do, I've had to do myself, in recovery, so they can't mess with that,' Jess agreed.

She confirmed the reports I'd been reading about the sharp increase in people interacting with eating disorder charities since Covid. It had been very noticeable in the therapy workshops she was running to help families affected by EDs.

'I did a workshop with a group of 16 people whose kids had all been diagnosed in lockdown. They hadn't had access to many services and were really poorly,' she said.

What she tends to find with some young people with disordered eating is that they miss out breakfast and lunch and then have dinner with their family to create a facade that everything is normal.

'But of course in lockdown, Mum and Dad were watching, which was good in a way because it's better if problems are picked up quicker, but then arguments within families have been more tricky because of the pressure of being under lockdown.'

The fallout of someone's eating disorder on other family members can't be overestimated.

'In terms of treatment, we probably do as much alongside families as with the people with eating disorders themselves,' Jess told me. 'For under-18s, there's an evidence-based treatment model, where we skill up families to implement a meal plan and take back control of all the food stuff going on in the house.'

In Dorset, where she is based, the NHS offers a four-day course of multi-family therapy for about eight families at a time. It's basically a crash course in eating disorders.

'People need skilling up really quickly because, ultimately, the presenting symptom, particularly with anorexia, is that people don't eat. So we've got to teach the families to get them to eat.'

It's not an easy task, even for therapists and clinicians, she added, but it's even harder when you're a parent worrying that your child is going to die.

'There's so much anxiety flying around and so many feelings, so we give families a lot of space and time to process that, and we look at how to reduce the anxiety and emotion for everyone,' Jess said.

I was reminded of something Laura had said to me: 'It's really, really difficult when people say to you, "Just eat. It's easy; it's simple," and actually it's really difficult.'

It's a dilemma: I understand what Laura was saying but there's a real need for urgency when people are so poorly that they're not eating. Before I spoke to Jess, I read about a famous clinical study of extended dietary deprivation conducted in 1944–5 at the University of Minnesota, which found that once someone goes into starvation, the brain structure changes.

Jess showed me a slide of a semi-starved brain, which had a huge gap where there should have been grey matter. She explained that if the body is not getting energy from food, it firstly burns fat, muscle and connective tissue and then starts to break down neurons in the brain, causing the grey matter to shrink.

'You might have heard that we don't often offer therapy if someone's below a certain BMI,' she said, 'and that's because half their brain's missing, really. The part of the brain that gets impacted is the rational part, so when family members say, "No part of this illness is rational!" I show them this picture and say, "That's because the part of the brain that would normally be rational has been starved. No one can be rational if this is happening to them because they haven't got the brain structure in place."'

I wanted to know if it's really that predictable. Does the same thing happen to everybody after three years of severe food restriction?

'It's a guideline,' Jess said. 'The brain is really plastic for the first three years,' she added, referring to the brain's ability to change and adapt to experience – 'but once it is starved for too long, it can't repair itself. If you don't catch someone within that window of three years, recovery rates tend to be six, seven or eight years. What's worrying is that a recent study by Beat has shown that, from symptoms to treatment, we're outside that window for most people in the

UK, which means that we're setting them up for a long, long road to recovery.'

Jess can't remember the time when she was at her lowest in weight, when she was in her late teens and struggling with anorexia. 'My mum can remember everything but I couldn't tell you anything that happened then.'

She had EDs from the ages of 11 to 21: it started with binge eating disorder; she slipped into anorexia when she found she was putting on weight and finally resorted to bulimia when she couldn't maintain control of her restricted diet. 'I've tried three different types of eating disorders and none of them were good,' she recalled wryly.

Although she was probably sick and tired of being asked the same old question, I asked what she thought was behind her issues with food.

'I think it was a combination of factors – and that's normally the case,' she said. 'Underlying it all is a really punishing self-hatred, low self-esteem and perfectionism. These tend to be the characteristics of people who get eating disorders, as well as what we call a "super-feeler nature", which describes really caring, intuitive and bright people who quite often take on other people's problems and see other people as more important than themselves.

'I had a bit of bullying in Year 6 and so my sense of self wasn't great when I made the transition from primary to secondary school. I moved to an all-girls grammar school and everything seemed to change: I felt completely unacceptable, overwhelmed by self-hatred and was self-harming at the age of 11, even though I didn't know what self-harm was. A darkness seemed to envelop me. I would say that there was quite a strong depression underlying the eating disorder.

'My dad had mental health issues, so my mum really struggled and I felt that supporting them and making myself useful would win me attention and praise. So I didn't really have that chance to emotionally grow myself because I was being a "parent", in a way. I wanted to look after everyone. That meant I wasn't telling anyone how I felt; I was keeping it all on the inside. That emotion has to go somewhere and in most cases a coping mechanism or a mental health issue will develop, and that's what happened.'

I told Jess about some of the girls I've met who said that, where they couldn't control certain areas, food was something they could control. 'How typical is that?' I asked.

'It's very typical of emotional distress,' she said. 'We know that people with eating disorders really struggle to express emotion and to read emotion in other people. So the world feels like quite a scary place; they don't feel in control very often and they don't necessarily know how to take care of themselves. So a lot of things can spin out of control, like relationships. "'So what can I control?" people think. "Food, and weight. Relationships aren't certain and neither are emotions: they're all very grey. Whereas eating disorders are all or nothing: I know where I stand with them."'

I wondered how much, in Jess's professional opinion, was down to genetics and how much circumstance.

'About two-thirds is genetics and personality,' she said. 'It's quite helpful for families to know this because there's a lot of guilt and blame within the family. Every family has issues; none of us are perfect, by any means. But it's often not only abusive or traumatised family homes where this is happening; it's also in really caring family homes. It seems to be in people with these traits of low self-esteem, perfectionism and a really caring personality.'

It took 18 months of counselling before Jess felt able to go through weight restoration. Until then, she wanted to be healthy but she didn't want to gain the weight. And it was a difficult process even when she decided to go for it: 'I refused to be weighed because although I knew I had to do it, I didn't want to think about it. "I'll keep eating. Just tell me when we get there," I said.'

Soon afterwards, she met her now-husband, whom she credits with being a big part of her recovery and helping her to learn to love herself.

She sees recovery in two parts. 'The first is the food. But then all the feelings come. Everything that you ran away from to go into the eating disorder is then back with you. Unfortunately, that's quite often where treatment ends, so you get discharged from treatment when you're a healthy weight but that's the most vulnerable time for recovery.'

In her therapy after weight restoration, she worked on managing emotions and negative thinking. 'I rewired my brain methodically with the truth and got rid of all the negativity. I worked really hard at it but it was worth it because, bit by bit, I became more free, more positive and fun – the best potential me I could be.'

The key areas she worked on were compassion for herself, self-care and getting rid of the tendency to be hard on herself. 'I refuse to let it even enter my brain now and that's probably the way I stay well and enjoy life. You've got to be superhuman to be able to not eat when you're starving. When I channelled that determination positively into life, I realised I could achieve great things. Now I've got three children and I juggle a million things, but I've got a lot of energy to bring to the world and I'm quite happy to do it because that energy needs to go somewhere.'

Jess set up a charity in Bournemouth, liaised with the NHS and went into the eating disorder service, setting up groups for people with EDs. Later, she studied in the evening to become a psychotherapist. One of the projects she is proudest of is an early intervention programme in a girls' school in Dorset, where there had been a lot of cases of eating disorders and children going into hospital. Jess trained up all the teachers, library staff and canteen staff to help spot early signs of eating disorders in the school community and discussed how policies in school could be amended to bring more awareness of eating disorders.

'Often, the person with an eating disorder themselves won't speak out or say, "I've got an issue,"' she said. 'It's quite often people around them who will spot these things before they recognise it themselves. We need to be the ones asking and if we're the ones asking, we need to know how to ask those questions and how to deal with those situations. People don't because they're worried they're going to make it worse.'

The project was so successful that the school has since had no hospital admissions, which is phenomenal. Jess has gone on to train school nurses and GPs throughout Dorset. She thinks we need more clarity about what to do and how to approach people who are struggling with EDs.

'Where there's a risk of suicide, people have learnt to ask, "Are you suicidal? Are you going to harm yourself?" We need that same directness with eating disorders because they are potentially just as dangerous. Anorexia has the highest mortality rate of any psychiatric disorder.'

Community awareness is key, in her opinion. 'For drugs and alcohol, we have loads of stuff going on in schools. Why not for eating disorders? It's such a common problem. It seems ridiculous that things are happening so slowly.'

I was interested to know whether Jess felt that full recovery was possible. 'Is it something you always have to manage or do some people get to a point where it's not an issue anymore?' I asked.

Research shows that nearly half of anorexia and bulimia patients fully recover. Jess counts herself in this number. 'There's this mentality that people can't recover from eating disorders but I was determined to fully recover because I didn't want to get better and still feel miserable,' she said. 'It didn't seem worth it. Why would I do that? I wanted to get rid of my fear and kept pushing for it. When I realised how hard it was, I just wanted to use my experience to help other people.'

She conceded that, 'There are some people who won't make a full recovery and for them recovery might mean planning their food still; it might mean that they've still got thoughts around body image that they can't shift.'

When you look into anorexia, the statistics are horrible. People die and there's a real lack of hope about recovery, so it was good to hear a positive message coming from someone like Jess. But although she grew up in a time when people knew so much less about EDs, she also struggled with her illness before social media and I wondered how much of a part she thought it played in people's illness and recovery.

I already knew that social media had played a large part in Laura's life and illness. When I first met her at the 136 suite, Laura had thousands of followers on Instagram, which felt to her like a place where she could express herself honestly and be accepted.

But it wasn't always a safe place. 'There is a very unhelpful side of the Instagram community where there's a lot of pro anorexia and pro self-harm,' Laura told me. 'I actually find when I'm relapsing, I get more followers, which can be hard, because then I feel like people only care when you're struggling.'

It's terrifying to hear that among the online community of people with eating disorders, there's a section known as pro-ana (anorexia) or pro-mia (bulimia), where people with eating disorders like anorexia and bulimia hand out tips on how to stay anorexic or bulimic. Extreme weight loss is celebrated and there are sites, blogs and chats centred around pictures of very underweight people. Some supporters of the pro-ana movement even post photos of themselves on Instagram attached to feeding tubes in hospital, while receiving treatment for an eating disorder. They wear their tubes like a badge of honour and are seen as 'good anorexics' among pro-ana followers on social media.

I'm curious about why there's been no legislation to restrict the online practices of pro-ana groups; it's so utterly heartbreaking … the idea that vulnerable people are being encouraged to starve themselves. It's hard to comprehend that Laura gets more likes and interaction on social media when she's ill or relapsed. It reinforces the eating disorder and gives the message that getting better is not the right thing to be doing, which is just so sad.

In France, a legal amendment was passed in 2015 giving authorities the power to punish anyone 'provoking people to excessive thinness by encouraging prolonged dietary restrictions that could expose them to a danger of death or directly impair their health.' But Mary George, a spokesperson for Beat, has said that the organisation would be against introducing similar measures in the UK. The view at Beat is that it wouldn't be helpful to criminalise the people behind the sites, who are very often struggling with EDs themselves. The charity would rather see the social media platforms and internet providers tackling the problem by removing and making it possible to report harmful content, although everybody recognises the difficulties involved with this. Ten years ago, when Instagram banned phrases such as 'pro-ana' and 'thinspiration' the content went on popping up under different names, often deliberately misspelled.

Jess estimated that about two-thirds of her patients visit pro-anorexia sites. Sometimes she'll have a session with someone where they go through them and block or unfollow them.

'Some of the people I've worked with will get added to some social media because they're known as a "good anorexic",' she said. 'People with tubes down their noses will get added because there's some kind of status to it. There are some amazingly positive accounts of recovery out there but some horrendous ones as well. We have to tackle it in treatment – and the National Institute for Health and Care Excellence (NICE) guidelines advise it – because there's no escape from it; it's such a big aspect of culture now.'

When I go about with people in their late teens and early twenties, I sometimes get the impression that people's online version of themselves is almost prioritised over their actual real life. So, if you're poorly and you put a whole level of something that isn't real on top of that and you've got strangers online saying, 'You look great!' it's no wonder you're going to start listening to those opinions.

The addictive draw of smartphones means that, even if someone has unfollowed pro-anorexia sites in therapy, when they're feeling low again there's every chance they'll have a quick scroll because the phone is in their hands almost 24 hours a day. If you think your eating disorder is the answer to managing your emotions, anything that pulls you in or justifies it can be just as addictive.

Jess said that some inpatients services take people's phones away from them. 'But of course, that's not the real world. We've got to learn how to manage what we do on our phones and taking things away doesn't necessarily help you learn how to do that. It's all about giving people the skills to make choices and recognise what will benefit your recovery or entrench your eating disorder more. That's what we're looking at all the time in therapy.'

I was mindful that I didn't want this to be a conversation with only females because I know that loads of males struggle with eating disorders, so I got in touch with James, a writer, eating disorders campaigner and researcher. James's recovery from anorexia and bulimia is still ongoing, 15 years after he developed anorexia as a teenager, while in treatment for OCD (obsessive-compulsive disorder). The team he was with at that time had very little knowledge of issues around food and there was no specialist service in Cardiff, where he was living, so he was only offered a full course of treatment for his eating disorder six years after it was diagnosed. By this time, it was entrenched and really difficult to deal with.

'It was such a missed opportunity,' he said. 'Had I have been helped then, in the right kind of way, I think that maybe I wouldn't still be struggling with bulimia now that I'm in my thirties. I've never fully recovered from the eating disorder.'

In his view, anorexia and bulimia are on a par in terms of risk and their effects on physical health. 'I've had a stomach tear as a result of bulimia and been in hospital as a result of bulimia just as often as with anorexia,' he said. 'I think bulimia gets overlooked because it can be so invisible, whereas when I was anorexic, everyone knew that I was really unwell. Though, because I'm male, people often thought I had cancer or there was something physically wrong, rather than anorexia. But with bulimia, it's completely invisible. I think that people assume that it's a lot less serious, whereas, actually, I find it just as much of a struggle.'

James's experience of eating disorders services as an adult has been less than positive and I wondered whether, as a male, he felt he was less likely to find the right help.

'I've often felt that people don't know how to talk to me about my body, my relationship with my body, my food and my eating,' he agreed. 'I've never worked with a male professional in treatment – I've only ever seen female members of staff – and in my whole time as an outpatient, I've only ever met one other patient who was male. There are things that are to do with my eating as a man, or my view of myself and my body and what my body should be like, that weren't reflected in the books or the leaflets that I was given. The clinics are quite feminised and it is a bit alienating if the only information you get about your body and the changes to your body is about your periods stopping or the impact on women's fertility. So I've felt like I've been in services run by women, for women. You don't want to be asking, "Where do I fit in here?" when you're already feeling excluded in other areas of your life. Or, "Who do I talk to about the fact that I feel I have to have a certain body because of the way that people might look at me on gay dating apps?" There was no space to talk about that kind of thing, which was actually a maintaining factor of my eating problems at one point. It's already a lonely experience to be isolated with your mental health. Then, if it's really difficult to connect when you do go for help, you can still feel even more out of reach.

'"What is it like to be male with eating disorders?" is a question I get asked a lot and I feel it's really complicated. When I speak about my experiences at an event or conference,

I feel I always have to be careful that I can't represent the male view because I'm just one male. One person's eating disorder could be completely different to somebody else's and the reasons why people have an eating disorder are so varied that the best thing you can do is listen to the individual person. Sex and gender are a part of the whole picture but they should never be used as a way to not look at the rest of the picture and think, "Well, what else is going on?"'

He has sometimes felt pigeonholed as a gay man. 'I think people have thought, "It's because you're gay and you haven't come to terms with being gay that you have an eating problem,"' he said. 'That's been a way of saying, "OK, this person has got sexuality issues and they'll grow out of it, so we don't need to give them treatment, or talk about it." It can be a way of writing somebody off and putting them in a box when, actually, being gay hasn't been an issue in itself for me. I come from a really liberal family and I don't relate to my friends who talk about how hard it was to come out. I feel that professionals have put that on me and said, "That must be why," when it was just really human issues about growing up, difficult times in school and difficult stuff in my family. I think it's much more about the person as an individual than their gender or their sex, which is just one part of the whole mosaic, isn't it?'

He has found it more helpful to take a more emotion-focused point of view of his illness. 'People have eating disorders for a reason, and they can serve a powerful function. For some people, eating disorders can be very effective at dealing with unaddressed needs, which is why people have them and they're so powerful. They can really fill in the gaps. I know that I have a strong need for connection and when I feel really disconnected or lonely then I'm more likely to fill that up with binge eating and vomiting, rather than being able to tolerate those emotions. I feel my feelings really strongly and sometimes it feels like I can't deal with that. So I jump out of the feeling into binge eating and vomiting – and with anorexia, it used to be extreme exercise and not eating – so that I don't have to feel that horrible feeling that I never learnt how to sit with. You're jumping out of the pain almost by enacting a physical pain, so you don't have to feel the emotional pain. Then afterwards, when I've been sick and am exhausted, I feel so much better. Even if it's temporary, it really, really works. I know that it's a very short-term thing because in the long term it's made me less and less tolerant of strong emotions because I know I can jump out of them. Lots of people will probably say, "Eating disorders are not about the food," but in my experience it has been *all about* the food, with food being the vehicle for dealing with whatever has been going on. There are so many different reasons why people have eating disorders.'

In treatment, James has been threatened with being sectioned if he didn't stop losing weight. 'But actually, what

I always really wanted was somebody to just sit with me and think about why I was doing it. It wasn't that I was broken or being badly behaved, even though the behaviours could be really dangerous. It was actually that I was in a lot of pain about lots of different things and I just didn't feel anybody was prepared to go there with me and look at that pain.'

He's not alone in thinking we need a huge upscaling of resources to help those currently suffering from EDs and to be able intervene in time when people start developing an ED. But it's also important to get the right kind of help: 'When you get help, it has to be good, it has to be useful. It's not enough for policies to say, "You must see somebody within eight weeks." It's what happens when you get there,' he said.

Compassion is also so, so crucial. 'People are trying the best that they can with the resources that they have. If the eating disorder is the best way, or the only way, you know how to cope, or it happens to be the thing that comes to hand at an important or difficult moment in your life that develops into a problem, then I just think, "Well done you for trying to get through." Yes, eating disorders are ultimately harmful, but having some way of coping can feel better than not being able to cope at all. I think we just need a lot of compassion for people who are doing their best. I was told, "You've just got to stop doing this bad thing," when I was just trying my best with the resources that I had. Nobody was helping me develop other skills to use instead, so I stayed with the ones I knew somehow worked.'

Overall, his message is a positive one, in that he believes it's absolutely possible to believe in recovery when it comes to your eating disorder, if you have encouragement and support to replace it with other things. 'Those things may be completely alien to you at first, but over time, and with encouragement, they will become more stable and healthier than using the eating disorder.'

I asked him what these things might be, aside from therapy for emotional regulation and past problems. 'Friends who I can ask for help without feeling ashamed or guilty,' he said. 'Having a supportive social network has been so important to me. It's not something that a doctor is going to prescribe you but my therapist helps me work on it and connecting with others has been just as important as trying to eat well. None of us can do without that.'

4

Recovering from Domestic Violence and Trauma

Natasha

When Natasha met John, she was in a good place. She had loads of friends, was modelling a bit, riding a lot and keeping herself ticking over, buying and selling horses. John came along and started bombarding her with text messages. He seemed caring and protective and showered her with compliments. 'I want to look after you,' he said. She thought she'd found the perfect boyfriend.

I met Natasha while researching the mental health impact of domestic abuse. She told me that she had grown up without much stability, often moving house and changing schools. Her home life was unpredictable: she describes her parents as 'very hands-off' and remembers a period of living without towels in the house. One year, her dad returned her Christmas presents on Boxing Day because he needed money to pay bills.

'I had to be resilient,' she told me. 'From a very young age, I had the mindset that I just had to get on with it and push through.'

She thinks her childhood experiences made her vulnerable to the sort of person who promises to look after you and take care of everything. She was 17, nearly 18, when she met John and a part of her craved the security he offered: he was 14 years older, with his own house, a car on finance and a nine-to-five job as a restaurant manager. He had a child from a previous relationship and gave the impression that he was a committed dad. He seemed solid and responsible in every way.

Within three months, she had moved in with him. A week later, he proposed. He was fun and attractive and they had great sex, so it was a while before she noticed how controlling he was. She felt flattered when he said, 'I want to support you,' and persuaded her to stop working. She went along with it as he slowly cut her off from her friends. 'The only reason people go out is to meet someone else,' he said. 'I love you. I'm all you need.'

At first, she said she enjoyed the intensity of the relationship. But as time went on, she felt trapped spending all day at home alone. Things came to a head about six months into living with him, when he tried to stop her from going out to meet her mum.

'When I argued back, he pointed to some intimate images on his phone that he had taken of me and said, "If you don't do what I say, I will send these pictures to your mum and show her what a little slut you are. And then I'll send them to everyone in your address book, including all your work contacts.'"

For Natasha, it was the moment that everything changed. And depressingly, a moment that felt all too similar to lots of other, separate moments that others have described to me.

Domestic abuse is very common in the UK. The figures are staggering: according to the Office for National Statistics (ONS), almost one in three women aged 16–59 will experience domestic abuse in her lifetime. In England and Wales alone, two women are killed by a current or former partner every week – a figure that, shockingly, hasn't changed for decades.

In the year ending March 2020, the ONS Crime Survey for England and Wales found that, based on police crime records and information from other organisations and support services, an estimated 1.6 million UK women experienced domestic abuse. It's unimaginable. And yet the charity Refuge says that calls and contacts to their 24-hour domestic abuse helpline rose around 60 per cent over the year following the first Covid-19 lockdown in 2020. The calls were from women being controlled, assaulted, stalked, harassed, abused and subjected to economic and tech abuse.

For this book, I wanted to know more about the mental health impact of living with an abuser, so I approached Lisa,

Refuge's director of communications and external relations at the time, for an overview.

'There is a massive overlap and intersection with domestic abuse and mental health,' Lisa told me. 'Women who experience domestic abuse are up to three times as likely to develop mental illness than women who don't experience it, so that's a pretty huge figure.'

Today we're hearing more about the many different forms of domestic abuse and I wondered if they could be contained within an overall definition.

'Domestic abuse is all about power and control and that manifests in many different ways,' Lisa explained. 'Most people identify it as broken bones and black eyes and the physical side of it. But actually, domestic abuse is when one person controls another in any way, be it physically, psychologically, emotionally, financially, economically and, increasingly, technologically. If you change your behaviour because you're frightened of your partner's reaction, you're experiencing domestic abuse.

'A common trait of perpetrators is to have a Jekyll and Hyde type personality. On the one hand, they're seemingly loving, caring, kind and look after you; on the other hand, they flip. So you're constantly walking on eggshells, uncertain of how your partner's going to react. That's why the consequences of domestic abuse are obviously huge on the physical person but also on the mental wellbeing.'

Since 2015, it has been a criminal offence to subject another person to coercive control, which is best described as a pattern of behaviour a perpetrator uses to gain power over their partner by eroding their autonomy and sense of self.

This is exactly what Natasha experienced while she was with John. 'There were so many ways that he tried to break me down and erase my identity,' she said.

From the start, he was jealous, possessive and acutely critical of her. He told her she was stupid, a bad person and a bad girlfriend. When she complained, he'd say, 'I never called you that,' or accuse her of overreacting and being dramatic. 'Why are you being like this? Other women don't behave like this.' She tried to be a better girlfriend but he never seemed satisfied.

He played games with her mind and constantly tripped her up. She'd bring him a drink and say, 'Here's your coffee.'

'No. I asked for a Coke.'

'You definitely asked for a coffee.'

'I didn't. I asked for a Coke.'

She started recording him on her phone so that when she got to the kitchen she could play back what he'd said and be sure of getting him the drink he asked for.

He used subtle intimidation to manipulate her. 'You're not going out in that, are you?' he'd say when she came downstairs after getting dressed.

'Why, what's wrong with it?'

He'd shrug. 'Oh, nothing, I was just asking.'

Sensing that he didn't like her outfit, she'd go back upstairs and change clothes.

He'd look surprised when she came downstairs again. 'Why have you got changed? What you were wearing was fine.'

'You basically said you didn't like it.'

'No, I didn't. I did not say that. Did I say that?'

'Well, no,' she admitted. 'You implied it, though.'

'Don't be silly. You're so stupid.'

So the next time it happened, she didn't go upstairs and change. But then he got angry. 'Are you going out looking like that? Like a slapper?' he said and she would be forced to change into something else.

'This sort of behaviour was soon routine. I accepted it. It became normal,' Natasha says. 'My good days were the days when he didn't berate me to a point of tears. I still find it very, very hard to cry because of his constant mocking. "You going to cry, are you? You're going to cry?" he'd taunt.'

The control stepped up when she fell pregnant two years into their relationship. Throughout the pregnancy, he starved her and withheld liquid for long periods. She wanted to leave him but believed him when he said she had nowhere to go. 'Nobody wants a single mother.'

'But you're starving me.'

'No one's going to believe you. You're damaged. It's all in your head.'

She was a size four for most of the time she was with him. 'A size eight is fat,' John told her. 'Remember, a size eight's fat.'

The resilience she had learnt in childhood kept her going but the pressure of constantly being told black is white and white is black took its toll. And there were days when she felt like she was living in a boot camp.

'He'd have me hoover four or five times a day. Just because,' she says.

'Go and hoover!'

'But I've already—'

'Go hoover. It's a fucking mess. There's dirt everywhere.'

'No, there's not.'

'He'd pick a tiny bit of fluff off the floor and say, "It's a mess. Do what I say."'

When she was a week overdue, she started haemorrhaging but he wouldn't allow her to call an ambulance; he made her wait an hour and a half until he got back from work and could drive her to the hospital. Eventually, her daughter Billie was born and she held her baby in her arms for the first time. 'Don't just stare at it,' he snapped, when Billie started crying. 'Shut it up.'

Life got steadily worse, especially as now she had her daughter to protect. She regularly thought about leaving but was so undermined by the abuse that she felt powerless. When she became pregnant with her son, Luke, a couple of years later, she lost hope of a way out; she got depressed, hit a low and had suicidal thoughts. 'I remember standing at the top of the stairs and thinking, I could just throw myself down the stairs right now.'

It is not unusual for a woman with an abusive partner to have these thoughts, according to Lisa at Refuge. 'There's a horrendous suicide statistic, which is that on average three women a week in the UK take their own lives to escape domestic abuse. So the death count is pretty horrific in this area, with two women being killed every week and three women a week killing themselves because that's the only option out that they can see.'

It almost doesn't bear thinking about how desperate and scared someone would have to be to take their own life in this situation but Lisa and her colleagues at Refuge have heard from women time and again that they feel there's no escape for them.

'Many women believe that the perpetrator will hunt them down and literally kill them and maybe their children too if they try to escape, so for some, tragically, their way of escape is to take their own lives,' Lisa said. 'That's why it's vital that we raise awareness of Refuge so women know that there are options and can reach out for support. No one should ever feel helpless and alone.'

The night Luke was born, John forced Natasha to leave hospital and come home just a few hours after giving birth. It was late and three-year-old Billie was tired. 'Shut the fuck up,' he snapped at the child. 'We already love the new baby more than we love you.'

He had no qualms about raping Natasha that night, even though he knew she'd had stitches after the labour. She was too scared of him to seek medical help despite the trauma this caused.

'What would I have said to the nurse? "Sorry, I sat on something." I couldn't have told the truth. There was such a fear there.'

So she just kept quiet.

'My reality was sitting at the breakfast table with a man who was like, "What have you got a face on for?" when he had raped me the night before and having to smooth over that resentment, confusion, hurt and just be like, "Nothing," to get through the day. You keep quiet so as not to have everything swept off the table or have him scream and shout at the little girl sat next to you. You do it to make it bearable – and the more you do it, the more you normalise it, and the more you normalise it, the more you live it.'

She was too ashamed to go to the police about the rape. She felt she would be judged or told it was her fault that it was happening. For a long while, she didn't even realise that what he was doing could be classed as rape because he was her partner, not some random stranger. Her shame increased when he filmed some of the assaults on her. Her self-esteem plummeted further.

'You get to a point where you can't turn off. Your dreams haunt you. Your day-to-day life haunts you. There are days when you think, I just don't know if I can do it anymore,' she said.

One Christmas, an abscess that had spread to her jawbone joint meant that for two weeks she couldn't open her mouth wider than to put a straw in. John wouldn't let her go to a dentist or even take a paracetamol.

'When you live with that sort of pain, the mental strain is immense,' she says. 'It's like having a screwdriver at your temple. You judge every single thing you do. If you drop something, you call yourself an idiot. You get so wound up. Since he used to mock me for crying, I had no way to express that emotion.'

I imagine it's easy to lose your perspective when you're going through this kind of torture. It's going to distort your thinking, isn't it?

'I remember lying in bed thinking about killing him, of going downstairs and getting a knife and sticking it in his throat,' she told me. 'Obviously, it's something that would never cross my mind now but in the frame of mind I was in, I wasn't afraid to do it. But then I'd think, I have no family, no friends: what would happen to my kids?'

One common tactic of a (male) abuser is to isolate a woman, reducing her contact with the outside world, groups and family members, making her more dependent on him and giving him more power over her.

'So many women experience mental health issues because they are isolated and controlled by their perpetrator,' Lisa explained.

'I wasn't scared of going to prison,' Natasha went on. 'I was already living in a kind of prison – and the odds were I wasn't going to get raped in an actual prison. But the thought of what would happen to my kids stopped me.'

One of John's most frequent threats was, 'If you leave me, I will get the kids and I will kill us and you will have to live with it.'

Warnings like this keep women trapped with their abuser. They are far less likely to kill their partners than be killed. 'My reality was coming out of there in a body bag,' Natasha said.

Once before, in 2014, she tried to leave John and go to her mum's house. The day before she made her second attempt to escape, one January morning in 2015, she was so terrified of what she was about to do that she rang the Refuge helpline to talk things through. 'The lady at Refuge saved my life by giving me the courage to go through with it.'

But the following morning, weeks of planning were nearly derailed as she walked away from dropping Luke off at pre-school. Suddenly, John appeared on the street before her. 'What have you got your bag for?' he asked.

She didn't need a bag because she wasn't allowed out of the house without permission. She couldn't travel anywhere unless he knew where she was going or was accompanying her. 'I was going to nip to town and sort out an issue at the council tax office,' she said quickly.

He paused and nodded. 'I'll drive you there.'

She tried not to show her dismay. After dropping Luke off, she had planned to walk to the police station in Horsham, where she had made an appointment to report John for abuse. Then she would collect the children from school and go straight to her mum's, taking a few overnight things in her bag.

But now John was checking up on her, as he so often did, and she was scared.

At the time, he worked for a Ford dealership, delivering cars to clients, and his job enabled him to pop home regularly between deliveries, putting her on constant high alert. Numerous times a day, he'd turn up at their house, park his car on the drive, walk inside and say, 'You all right?'

'Yes,' she'd say.

'What you doing?' he'd ask.

'Not a lot,' she'd reply, keeping her tone even, knowing that if she questioned why he was there, or complained, he would kick off.

Now, as he drove her into Horsham, she had no idea whether or not he believed her council tax story. Would he wait for her outside the council office, or go? She knew he had a car to deliver.

She felt his eyes follow her as she got out of the car and entered the building. She hesitated. 'You OK?' a woman asked.

'Yes, can you just talk to me for a second?' she said, her heart pounding. 'I'm going to sit down.'

'OK,' the woman said, clearly sensing something was amiss.

Natasha kept talking until she saw John's car pull away, then leapt to her feet. 'Thank you, bye!' she said hurriedly to the woman and rushed out of the building.

Knowing that John could drive past at any second on his way back to the dealership, she ran as fast as she could in the direction of the police station, across the park in the centre of Horsham and along the main road.

'I was running in absolute fear, thinking, "If he finds me on this road, there is absolutely no logical reason for me to be here. He's going to know."'

When she made it to the police station, she began the process of applying for a non-molestation order against him.

'Is there anything else you want to tell me?' the police officer asked her, after he had taken the details down.

She burst into tears. 'He constantly rapes me. I have no rights over my body. I can be asleep, I can lay there and ignore him, I can tell him he makes me sick, I can punch him, but he will carry on regardless,' she said. 'And I just can't live like this anymore.'

Later that day, John was arrested and released on bail.

Natasha never considered going back to John again, even though living with her mum became impossible because of problems with her mum's partner and she faced difficulty and uncertainty when she was housed in a refuge in Portsmouth. One of the many things that stopped her returning was the thought of how damaging his behaviour was to Billie and Luke.

'About two weeks before I left him, I got a bit rebellious and said, "My pillow is absolutely screwed and I'm not sleeping, so I'm just going to nip to Tesco to get a new one – and I'm going whether you like it or not,"' she recalled.

'No, you're fucking not, you slut,' John shouted.

Billie, aged five, stood up on the dining room chair and said, 'You are not going to call my mummy that word!'

'Sit back down before I smack you in the mouth,' he yelled at her and Billie ran upstairs and cried.

'I went absolutely mad,' Natasha told me. 'I remember thinking, "If he can talk to her like that and she knows it's wrong at five, I'm setting my daughter up to either accept that behaviour or perpetrate that behaviour. I'm setting my son up to accept it or create it, and I cannot do that to the world. I have a responsibility."'

According to information on the Royal College of Psychiatrists' website, based on various studies and collated in 2015, 'Children who have witnessed violence and abuse are more likely to become involved in a violent and abusive relationship themselves.'

As Natasha feared, research has found that some boys will learn from their fathers or other male figures close to them to be violent towards women and some girls will learn to accept and put up with male violence – although many more will reject what they have seen and won't repeat the pattern. Other possibilities in the short and long term include children experiencing anxiety, depression, addiction issues, eating disorders and self-harming.

I'm also mindful of the findings of a 2017 government study in which 57 per cent of women in prison reported having experienced domestic violence and more than 50 per cent recalled emotional, physical or sexual abuse as a child. Often they had been at the receiving end of far more serious crimes than they had committed. This is something I saw a lot with the girls I spent time with in US prisons.

Fortunately, Natasha did not go back. She was given social housing and within a few weeks, she met Ben, her current husband, who has supported her through physical illness and the mental fallout of spending eight years in an abusive relationship. But her troubles were far from over. Three months later, she had a mini-stroke and lost the use of the right side of her body for ten months. Six years on, she still can't feel one side of her face. The stroke led to horrifically painful headaches known as hemiplegic migraines, which are characterised by weakness down one side of the body, numbness and visual impairment.

'I would have uncontrollable pain through my nervous system,' she told me. 'I'd be shaking and my hands wouldn't grip; my knuckles used to dislocate. I also had Prinzmetal angina, which is chest pain caused by spasms in a coronary artery that narrows it and reduces the blood flow to your heart.'

She believes her health problems are a direct result of the years she spent living constantly with adrenaline. 'I was in fight-or-flight mode day and night,' she explained. 'There was no let up from the stress.'

She told me that she no longer has natural responses to physical pain. Her nerves are extremely sensitive: the agony of a banged elbow might last all day; the cat could scratch her and the pain could keep her up all night. Five of her teeth are rotted to the gum and need to be removed. Her jawbone is black under the skin. She wears a morphine patch to deal with her nerve pain.

She thinks the trauma of the rapes presented as a kind of physiological post-traumatic stress disorder (PTSD). 'I heard the head of Hampshire police say recently that rape is the most serious crime you can survive, and it's true. And because I was trying to be OK for my children while I was living with a rapist and abuser, I buried the trauma so deep that it was coming out in my body.'

Several studies have shown that living with long-term stress and elevated cortisol, the stress hormone, can cause anything from headaches to thyroid disorders and depression, among other conditions.

'After I left him, I had days when I couldn't sit up in bed. It was absolutely horrific, I was so ill. I couldn't walk down the stairs without having to sit down. Some days, I'd do the school run, come back, sit with my back against the front door and break my heart for half an hour because it hurt so much. I'd have knee braces on, I'd have hand braces. It would just be ridiculous.'

She was terrified of being stalked by John and fearful that he would follow the children. She was constantly looking over her shoulder when she did the school run and the school office had a photo of him up on the wall, in case he tried to abduct them.

Ben, who understood what it was like to live with an abusive partner, supported her and the children throughout. The day after she had the mini-stroke, he suggested they relocate to the north of England and move in together, which they did. When she started to recover her health, he suggested having a baby; they went on to have George, who is now five. When she was pregnant, they agreed to get married. It was an unexpected happy ending for Natasha, who had assumed she would be bringing her children up as a single mum.

But she never fully escaped her ex. He harassed her constantly, often by contacting her friends and family, and talked people she had never met into reporting her to the police for mistreating Billie and Luke.

'A woman from Berkshire said she'd seen me in Nottingham punching Billie in the face,' she says. 'Honestly, the police would be at the door all the time. It was horrendous.

In the end, they marked us down as: unless it's a 999 call, they're not coming out.'

When she was pregnant with George, a woman she didn't know started posting threatening videos on Facebook. 'She was going to find me, she was going to kick my baby out of me, she was going to ruin my life and she was going to make sure Ben paid for what I've done to John.'

Natasha was running an equestrian magazine online at the time and John started posting things about her on Facebook. 'He befriended a woman in Scotland who was really vulnerable but also a loudmouth and rough as hell, and she started putting videos on about me and about my business. It ruined the business. They posted that I was cruel to animals.'

She has kept a baseball bat in her bedroom since that time, just in case she ever has to use it to defend herself. 'Come at me!' she says defiantly. 'Because I'm not the person I was. I'm not the person he bullied and broke down and degraded.'

I'm in awe of how Natasha manages to stay resilient. She seemed happy and strong when I spoke to her at the close of 2020: her marriage was great and her health improved. To look at her, you wouldn't know anything was wrong (a cliché, I know). 'But even today, I have my good days and my bad days. I mean, yesterday was a bad day. I probably slept about 16 hours yesterday in total.'

She says she was 'skeletal' when she left the relationship with her ex and although she ate well, couldn't put on weight.

It wasn't until John was sent to prison in March 2018 that her metabolism balanced out and she began to look healthy again. But first she had to get through the court case.

'So, we went to court and I got cross-examined for six and a half hours, which, I'm not going to lie, was quite traumatic, the main point probably being that the prosecution barrister implied that going to bed naked was a signal that it's OK to be raped,' she told me.

John was up for four charges of rape and one of assault by penetration, and he was found guilty of three charges of rape and one of assault by penetration.

'The only reason that the first charge was discounted was because I couldn't give a definitive start date for the rape,' Natasha explained. 'The judge gave him the maximum sentence that can be given, which is 15 years. He was given 12 custodial and 3 on licence, which really is fantastic.'

Natasha was given a lifetime restraining order against her ex and thought that would be the end of it. John went quiet for most of his first year in prison and, in the light of the conviction, Ben felt it was a good time to apply to adopt Billie and Luke, who already called him dad. But when a social worker got in contact with John to inform him of the application, he applied for access to the children in order to block the adoption.

The first court hearing was in February 2019. When Natasha and Ben walked into the court room, Ben stood in front of her, pointed at a camera and said, 'Is that off?'

The court clerk said, 'Well, no.'

'It needs to be off. She doesn't want to see him,' Ben said.

'Is there a problem?' the court clerk asked Natasha, as if he thought that perhaps Ben was playing the macho partner who doesn't want his wife communicating with her ex.

'Yes, he raped me,' Natasha said.

The clerk blanched and straightaway went to the judge, who ordered the cameras turned off.

'John sat there on camera going, "Oh, look at them acting up. She's got to play the victim, hasn't she? Got to have a bit of sympathy,"' Natasha recalled. 'It makes you feel like rubbish, you know. Just hearing his voice was violating.'

During the hearing, John falsely claimed that Natasha was being investigated for abusing Billie and Luke. Natasha's heart sank. Even in a court of law, she said, he was lying about her and trying to gaslight her.

'The rational part of me is saying, "Don't be so silly," and another part of me is thinking, "What sort of moron would lie in a court of law?" But I also had my head in my hands, thinking, "Oh God."'

During the hearing, the judge questioned the practicality of John's application for access to the children. 'I mean, where were they going to stay when they went to see him? Under his bed in his cell?' Natasha says.

The following day, she discovered that he had been repeatedly calling Dorset and Sussex police to report her for coercive control and assault during their relationship. At the next hearing, he underlined these allegations and said that a prison counsellor had helped him to realise that he'd been abused by Natasha while living with her. It was a ludicrous claim that the police didn't entertain for one minute but she couldn't help getting depressed about it. 'I felt like John was taking ownership of it again and it made me really miserable.'

Billie, 11, and Luke, 8, were called up to do a video call with the court officer. 'They're very confident kids in general but they both broke down, hysterically crying, and refused to talk to the screen,' Natasha told me. 'It just really wounded them.'

Speaking to Natasha, I could tell that her children had gone from being in a really unhealthy, abusive household to a space where they're adored and safe and happy. She and Ben were super happy when the adoption went through in 2021. Having done everything she could to shield them from the abuse and unhappiness of the relationship with John, she clearly worries about them and their mental health is a sensitive subject.

'When we first moved, Billie found it very hard that we were all of a sudden surrounded by people,' she says.

Billie was used to living in isolation because John wouldn't let them go out. She went on to have anger outbursts that reminded Natasha of her ex. She threw her stuff down the stairs and refused to go to bed. It put a strain on Natasha and Ben's relationship.

'Luke had to be carried everywhere because he was so afraid of everything. If you didn't, there were massive tantrums but I couldn't carry him; it was making me ill,' she adds.

'When we had George, everything calmed down hugely. The only trouble came when we had visits from Cafcass (Children and Family Court Advisory and Support Service). Billie wrote letters to the judge, saying, "My dad is Ben Saunders. I won't mention the other man's name. Thank you, your Honour. Please let me be adopted." Luke wrote an A4 page breaking his heart about how dads are loving and caring and like Bourbon biscuits and that's how he knows Ben is his dad. And how he never wants to see John because he scares him and hurts Mum.'

When Natasha and I spoke, Luke was struggling to come to terms with learning that Ben isn't his biological dad. 'It shattered his world because he only vaguely remembers a time before Ben.'

The family's social workers advised Natasha to tell Luke that his dad is in prison because he's a bad person. 'So now, if he does even the slightest thing wrong, he gets really worried, "Am I a bad person?" he asks. "Am I going to grow up to be a bad person?" I explain to him that he's a wonderful person. "People are not born bad. You make bad choices and even if you make bad choices, you can atone for them. You can become a good person. But some people only want to make bad choices, whether it's influences from their childhood, or whatever. Unfortunately that's the case with him but you're not a bad person."'

Most nights before bed, Luke asks questions about prison. He wants to know how the cells look and what the food is like. He wants to know if John will be monitored when he's released and where he will go.'

John has since tried to appeal his conviction after over two years in prison.

'Luke wants me to promise him that John won't have any pets when he's released because he remembers him kicking our dog around the kitchen and me getting in front of it and him then kicking me. He wants me to promise to tell any woman who dates him what he's done and who he is, and to make sure that he knows he hates him.'

After a couple of issues came up at school, Luke had an appointment to see the school counsellor to talk about his feelings, but since the adoption went through, both he and his sister are 'like different children', Natasha says happily.

As for Natasha, she's such an incredible survivor and, despite her PTSD, seems to have recovered her sense of self and bubbly personality. Still, she said, there's a residual anxiety from living with her ex that Ben will suddenly flip and turn into a monster, even though he never has. When she had a tyre puncture on their car and was late home recently, she had a moment of feeling terrified that Ben would be furious with her. Back at home, he said, 'I'm so glad you're back safely. Are you all right?' and gave her a hug.

'But the fear was still there,' she said. 'It takes a long time after you leave to drop those habits. For instance, if a name pops up on my phone that he doesn't know, I still feel I have to explain who it is and justify it.'

'I told you about it; I did tell you!' she'll protest.

'It's fine,' Ben says. 'Don't worry about it.'

She is determined to recover fully from her experiences, mentally and physically, and is a powerful campaigner against domestic abuse. 'I settled for eight years. I watched the world go by. I watched everybody live their lives while I trod water, I lived for bedtime for eight years. You know, I got up and I went to sleep. That was it. So now I've got so much I want to do,' she told me.

She now gives lectures on domestic abuse to the Metropolitan Police, is taking tentative steps towards standing for Parliament and does all she can to raise money for Refuge, the charity she credits with saving her life. She has halved her morphine patch and is hoping to get off it completely. Pets kept running in and out of view while we were speaking. She is married to a man who she describes as 'my best friend and my biggest champion'. Her children are safe and loved.

5

Postnatal Illness

Dani and Danielle

We're told, aren't we, that having a baby is supposed to be a time of joy and deep connection, but for some new mums, things don't go as expected. Everybody's telling them how lucky they are. They know they should be thinking, 'How wonderful this is!' And yet they're not feeling it.

It's a huge life change (well, so I'm told, though what would I know?!). Newborns require a lot of care and attention; they feed every two to four hours, day and night; they need changing, bathing, soothing and cuddling, and it can feel as if there's not a lot of time left in the day to do anything else. It's not surprising if a first-time mum feels exhausted at times, or a bit down about their sudden change in lifestyle, or their lack of freedom. Throw financial difficulties or worry about the baby's health into the mix and the first few weeks after a birth can be as anxious as they are fulfilling.

Sometimes, though, the pressures of those first few days and weeks can lead to depression, often without anyone realising. With all the other changes going on during this time, it's probably quite hard to recognise what is and isn't 'normal' in terms of what you're feeling. So it's helpful to know that at least one in ten mothers develops postnatal depression (PND) in the year after their baby is born. And like all forms of depression, PND can be mild, moderate or severe, and can develop gradually or suddenly.

It's not known exactly what triggers PND but research shows that it could be caused by anything from a traumatic delivery to a sudden drop in hormones after giving birth. People with a history of depression and other mental health issues are thought to be more prone to it, although they won't necessarily experience it; depression during pregnancy, bereavement and environmental stress can also be factors. Sometimes there's no obvious reason for it at all.

Curious to know more about PND and other mental health issues that people can experience after having a baby, I approached a couple of the leading UK postnatal illness charities for information. Through PANDAS, the UK charity offering support and awareness to people affected by PND, I met Dani, a lovely nurse from Lancashire, who was 24 when her first child, Annabelle, was born.

Dani experienced the onset of PND very suddenly. She vividly remembers a moment when she was sitting on the sofa trying to breastfeed Annabelle, three days after the birth.

'I lost all emotion,' she told me. 'I just had nothing to give her. It's scary to say now but I absolutely hated her. I thought she'd ruined my life.'

Stuck at home while her husband was out working two jobs, Dani felt lonely, isolated and resentful – the opposite of what you'd expect to be feeling as a first-time mum. She didn't realise that she was experiencing PND. Her feelings felt absolutely real to her.

'I kept thinking, "What's happened? What has my life come to? Who is this person who now just absolutely needs me? Where's my mothering instinct? How am I meant to love her and raise her feeling like this?" It was horrible because I had always wanted children; I had always been a very maternal person. Yet suddenly I had these thoughts going through my head. There was no rationality to it at all.'

Dani can trace her PND journey back to before she even knew she was pregnant with Annabelle. After being constantly sick for nearly a week, she had gone to see her GP thinking she had gastroenteritis. The nausea had started mid-air, she explained, as she'd plunged thousands of feet towards the ground while doing a sponsored parachute jump a few days earlier.

Her doctor sent her for tests at her local hospital, where it was discovered that she was seven weeks pregnant. But amid the flurry of activity and concern among the medical staff around her severe nausea and vomiting and the impact it might have on her baby, no one actually told her she was pregnant or discussed the implications with her.

'That's where my anxiety started, really, because it was all so unknown,' she recalled. 'I was young, I had no idea what was going on and I was feeling dreadful.'

Dani had such severe morning sickness (known medically as hyperemesis gravidarum) that she was only able to work on and off during the pregnancy.

'One doctor told me later that when I jumped out of that plane, I had a massive rush of adrenaline and my body threw everything it could into keeping Annabelle alive. The surge of hormones made me sick for the next 14 weeks.'

Not being able to work meant that she and her husband Dave couldn't afford their own place and had to live with Dani's parents. Eventually, they moved but with Dave off working two jobs, she rarely saw him. She had a lonely few months and then the baby's birth was stressful: Annabelle was born with the umbilical cord wrapped around her neck and nearly died.

Three days later, Dani's mood plunged and she stopped feeling any connection with Annabelle.

'Breastfeeding was utter hell after that because I had no bond with her at all,' she said. 'After two weeks, I decided that I couldn't do it anymore and it felt like such a fail. When the nurses at the weigh-in clinic saw that I was giving her formula, there were tuts and hisses, and comments like, "So you couldn't carry on? You couldn't try harder; you couldn't persevere?"

'In fact, I had no issues with breastfeeding and she was feeding fine; it was just having her close to me that was hard. I actively sought out people who would give her cuddles so that I didn't have to hold her – I drove far and wide to visit people who would open the door and say, "Give her here! I'll feed her for you. You go and have a hot brew."

'It was awful when we stayed at home: she'd be crying for hours in her Moses basket, even though I'd fed her and changed her, and I'd be crying because I didn't know what she wanted. Of course, she just wanted me.'

Dani didn't tell anyone how she was feeling. Like the majority of parents experiencing PND, she was too scared to open up and admit that she hadn't bonded with Annabelle. Images of perfect mums are always around us – online, on telly, on magazine covers and Christmas calendars – so maybe it's society's idealised view of motherhood that sometimes prevents women from asking for help if they're struggling, especially the younger mums.

'They feel they shouldn't say anything, or perhaps they're not sure how to express how they're feeling, or who to turn to,' said Michelle, the safeguarding officer at PANDAS.

Michelle explained that PND is different from the 'baby blues', a brief, mild depression that many mothers experience after giving birth, when they might feel down and tearful for a day or two, or temporarily overwhelmed.

'PND is more of a feeling you have every day, that you can't shake, and you think, "Why am I feeling this?"' Michelle said.

For mums who have tried desperately to have a baby and perhaps had IVF, it can be really hard to say that things aren't going well after a longed-for child arrives. Or maybe they don't even realise what's happening because PND can creep up gradually, or they don't know it exists and so don't recognise what is happening to them, or they're scared their baby will be taken away from them if they're not a good enough parent.

Dani was fortunate that her community midwife noticed something was wrong on her final visit. When she asked Dani, 'How are you feeling?' and Dani said, 'I'm fine!' the midwife rolled her eyes at Dave, shook her head and said, 'We'll be back tomorrow.'

The following day, a health visitor arrived with a mental health screening tool: a set of ten questions that can flag up signs of depression in pregnant women and new mums.

Dani's score indicated that she was moderately depressed and the health visitor arranged an appointment with her GP.

'And then I was sent through this amazing whirlwind of support,' Dani recalled. 'It was almost like someone put a massive blanket around me. This was ten years ago when the Sure Start children's centres were opening up and you could access the services free of charge. I had everything from peer support and counselling to medication.'

Dani worked hard at her recovery and, in the process, found her calling and began to train as a nurse. Meanwhile, she and Dave put a lot of thought into whether to try for another child, she said. Could they risk going through PND again? They decided to go for it and when Dani eventually fell pregnant with Isaac towards the end of her nursing training, she felt confident that she could cope, if it happened.

'And that's where I was very, very wrong,' she said. 'My pregnancy with Isaac was plain sailing, the birth was plain sailing – and then it hit me like a ton of bricks. It wasn't like the first time: this was a feeling of absolute hopelessness. There was just no hope in anything.'

It was not being able to breastfeed Isaac that tipped her over the edge, she thinks. 'I felt I'd failed Annabelle and I wanted to make it right the second time around, but I couldn't. I thought, "I'm not a good enough mum. I can't give my child breastmilk, the most natural, precious gift in the world."'

By this time, Dani and Dave had moved to Merseyside, which seemed like a world away from where they'd lived in Lancashire, in terms of postnatal care. 'Even though I'd been diagnosed with postnatal depression with Annabelle, there was nobody looking out for me this time. The midwives and health visitors came and went: nobody asked me, "How are you feeling?"'

Obviously, Dani was alert to the possibility that she might experience PND again but explained that when you're in the thick of it, you don't realise it's happening. 'There was no voice in my mind that said, "Hang on a minute, Dani, this isn't you. This isn't how you would act. You've been through this before."

'With depression, as with other mental health issues, you don't know you've got a problem until it bites you in the arse, basically,' she said. 'Your brain has been sucked dry of serotonin and you're not yourself.'

It was only when Dave and a couple of her closest friends gave her a nudge that she asked for help. 'But there didn't seem to be any,' she said, 'and I thought, "If there was something wrong with me mentally, the doctors would want to help, so I must be feeling this way because I'm not good enough at doing what I'm doing."'

Dani reached her lowest point when Isaac was five months old. 'I was at home alone one night and I felt I couldn't go on. The children were asleep and Dave was working late – I got all the medication that I could find, all your paracetamol pills and your painkillers, and laid them out on the bed. Then I got myself a drink and just sat there and stared at the pills, thinking, "There's just nothing else for me to do. I've asked for help. Nobody's here for me. I can't do this anymore."'

Tragically, suicide is the leading cause of death in mothers in the first year after their child is born. According to statistics quoted by the suicide prevention charity Papyrus UK, one in nine maternal deaths in the UK is as a result of suicide, and Dani came close to being among them. I can't imagine how desperate she must have been feeling to seriously consider taking her own life.

But then, just as she was about to take the array of pills on her bed, something happened to make her pause for one crucial moment: baby Isaac woke up and started crying.

'He was not long fed, so I knew he wasn't hungry. I thought, "Well, I can't just leave him crying because then the neighbours are going to wonder what's going on and the pills won't have enough time to work and I'll get saved." So I went over to try to shush him. And he smiled.

'I don't know why he smiled – it was probably just seeing his mum, to be fair – but suddenly I realised, I am all he needs. It doesn't matter how my mind's working, it doesn't matter what's happening – he needs his mum; he wants his mum; he is clearly smiling at his mum.'

She threw away the pills and picked up Isaac for a cuddle. 'For the first time, I felt a connection with him,' she said. 'I thought, "This is my son – and this is how it's meant to be." I didn't start particularly getting better at that point but it was the turning point. I realised: no, I need to get better, for my kids.'

Dani didn't find CBT very helpful (though many other new mums do). Antidepressants had more of an impact on her recovery but she thinks that what helped her most was learning more about PND and being supported by friends and people who'd had similar experiences. When Isaac was three, she got involved with PANDAS and started a PND support group for other mums. Listening to everybody's stories shone a light on how many missed opportunities there had been along the way for healthcare workers to help the mums in her group, either because they weren't equipped to recognise they were struggling or they hadn't asked the right questions.

Dani single-handedly organised an awareness-raising event with guest speakers at her local library and invited mums and representatives from all the perinatal services in Merseyside and Cheshire. Two years later, she repeated the event and this time felt confident enough to stand up and be one of the speakers. She told her story from beginning to end in front of 55 service providers and mums. It was another turning point in her recovery.

'I thought, "You know what? This is the best way to get the information out there, so that the professionals can properly support people who are feeling like I felt."'

Dani is now the group and training manager at PANDAS and uses her experience of PND to help others recover from the illness. 'One of the things I always say to parents is, "It's not you; it's the illness. If you were to take away the depression, you would not be talking or acting in that way."'

When she had her third child, Eleanor, Dani didn't experience depression, but thinks that if she had, being older, she would have felt more confident about speaking out and asking for help sooner. 'Our aim at PANDAS is to get the experiences out there and talked about, to remove the stigma around PND. Then mums will feel they can reach out when they're starting to feel unwell – rather than leaving it until they reach the depths of despair – and we can equip them with the tools and resources to go and get support as early on as possible. It's all about recognising the signs and knowing who to contact for advice and help.'

Like PND, postpartum psychosis (PP) is another postnatal illness that may not be easy to spot in its early stages because people don't always pick up on unusual behaviour amid the massive changes that come with having a baby. But although it's rare, affecting one in a thousand women, PP is potentially much more serious than PND if it goes unrecognised.

Also known as puerperal psychosis, it usually appears within a month of giving birth and should be treated as a medical emergency.

The charity Action on Postpartum Psychosis (APP) put me in touch with Danielle, a midwife living in South Wales, who was happy to talk me through the lead up to the temporary psychosis she experienced in 2017.

Danielle describes herself as 'normally very relaxed and bubbly' and she had a happy, healthy pregnancy, she told me, although there was a bit of anxiety because she'd had a miscarriage shortly before getting pregnant this time. Ideally, she would have liked a home birth, or even a water birth, but when her baby went 12 days over its due date, she resigned herself to giving birth in the labour ward of the hospital where she worked.

Her partner Darren took her to the hospital. Her life was never the same again.

'I remember going into the delivery room and I feel as if I didn't walk out of the room the same person,' she said.

The birth was fraught with anxiety. Being a midwife and knowing what could go wrong made things worse. 'It was very hard for me to switch off and be the mum in that room,' she said.

Among other things, her epidural (an anaesthetic injection into the space around the spinal nerves in the back) didn't work properly, so she was in a lot of pain. When the epidural was eventually topped up, the coverage went so high that it made her feel like she couldn't breathe and it caused stiffness in her neck.

'I was frightened to death about that,' she said. 'I hadn't wanted an epidural because I know it comes with complications.'

After a night spent in labour, she had a C-section – but during the operation, the epidural became less effective and she started to have sensation. It was one nightmare after another: after she was anaesthetised again, she began to bleed heavily.

'Initially, I wasn't that concerned,' she recalled, 'but then I heard them ask for a strong drug to contract the uterus, which made me think, "Oh my God, it must be bad."'

She lost just under 1.5 litres of blood. It wasn't a major haemorrhage but of course it was frightening.

The whole experience sounds terrifying and exhausting. At least she had her healthy, new baby to distract her. 'It's very true what they say: when you see your baby for the first time, you think, I'll go through that 100 times to have this baby,' she said. 'It was afterwards that I kept going over it and asking, "Why did all these things happen?"'

The following two days in hospital were filled with family and colleagues popping in to see her and baby April. By now, though, there were signs that Danielle wasn't doing too well.

'When everyone came to see me, I couldn't say, "Look at my beautiful baby in her cot." It was, "You'll never guess what happened to me! I had a haemorrhage …"'

Assuming she was worn out, her visitors were full of sympathy and no one picked up on her growing depression.

Three days after the birth, she was glad to go home. As she stepped through the door, she saw the family dog, their good-natured husky, wagging its tail in excitement. It's her first memory of things not being right.

'Why is she looking at us like that?' she asked Darren nervously, backing away from the dog.

'What do you mean?' he said.

'Why does she look like she's going to attack us?'

She took to shielding April's cot with her body whenever the dog was in the room.

I can imagine that all your feelings can be heightened when you've just had a baby but I wondered if she thought it was unusual to catastrophise in this way, especially as she had been looking forward to introducing April and the dog.

'Definitely, especially as I've always been a dog person,' she said. 'My mum has always had massive dogs and, as children, she would lie us out on the settee and let the dogs sniff us. That was a ritual whenever we had new additions to the family and I was looking forward to carrying on the tradition with my baby.'

That night, she couldn't get to sleep. 'No matter how tired I was, I just couldn't shut off at all,' she said. 'I kept replaying everything that had happened at the birth over in my mind. I was still hurting from the section, still bleeding quite heavily; I really felt like I'd been knocked over by a bus and thought, "Is this normal? Is this what it's supposed to be like?"'

A steady stream of people came to see her but instead of cooing over the new baby and chatting about sleep patterns and feeding, all Danielle could talk about was what a horrific time she'd had with the birth. 'I needed to let people know,' she said. 'It seemed essential that they couldn't leave the house until I'd told them exactly what had happened.'

She was revisiting the horror of the birth with different visitors at least three times a day. 'A lot of these people weren't midwives and so I had to go into detail to explain everything – otherwise it wouldn't make sense – so the stories would just go on and on and on,' she said.

Again, everybody was sympathetic. 'That sounds terrible. What a rough time you've had,' they said, while trying to steer the conversation back to the baby. 'Isn't she lovely?'

She thinks that the community midwives and the health visitor who came to check on her and the baby didn't pick up on her distress because she put on a front that she was coping well. Also, she knew them through her job and they talked about her experiences from a work perspective. 'It's very normal for two midwives to get together and say, "I had this and I had that and they did this ..." and so I think that's why people didn't really think my behaviour was that unusual at the time,' she said.

She didn't have any trouble looking after April. She was so thorough with her four-hourly feeds during the night that, after feeding, changing, winding and settling the baby, there were only ever a couple of hours left before the next feed. Her sleeplessness got worse. She became so overtired that she couldn't relax; she lay in the dark, wide awake for the hours between feeds. She grew petrified that she wasn't sleeping. One night she Googled whether sleep deprivation could kill you. 'I look back and think, "That's absolutely crazy,"' she said.

She began to feel resentful towards Darren because he had no trouble sleeping. He offered to do the night feeds for her but she said, 'Don't worry, I'll probably be awake anyway; I'll do it.'

Her appetite was off and she couldn't finish her food; she resented Darren because he could. She started writing down her feelings because she knew something wasn't right but kept telling herself it was the baby blues or a bit of PND, which she knew about through her job.

One night, while she was talking to Darren about PND, she said, 'And there's something much, much worse called puerperal psychosis ...'

'What happens if you have that?' Darren asked.

'It can get so bad that mums don't bond with their baby or they harm their baby or themselves. But you don't need to worry, I definitely don't feel like that!'

It was as if she knew subconsciously what was going on but was too much in the thick of it to detach and self-diagnose.

'Then things started to get weirder,' she said.

Smells became really vibrant and intense, and when she couldn't sleep, she started going downstairs in the middle of the night and doing a wash with her favourite strawberry fabric conditioner, then turning on the heating so that the strawberry smell would fill the house.

She decided that repeating the story of the birth in detail was making her ill and began to lay down complicated rules for visitors about what they could and couldn't ask her, instructing Darren to police the conversations and censor what he said to people, including his own parents. Darren has since said he thought it was odd behaviour but he didn't want to upset someone who'd just had a baby when their emotions were all over the place.

I can see why he was so cautious. It's all unknown territory – if you've never had a kid before, you don't know if it's typical to feel this way, or for your partner to behave in a certain way.

Danielle became obsessed with becoming a mum blogger and started leaving negative reviews about baby products in the middle of the night.

'April wasn't the easiest to feed and I was directing all my frustration and anger at the companies making the products that didn't work for me personally, and I was doing it at stupid o'clock in the morning, when I couldn't sleep,' she said.

'When I look back at what I wrote, you can see the chaos in what I was writing.'

Thirteen days after April was born, Danielle decided that she and Darren were arguing too much and that he needed to leave because she didn't want any negativity around her daughter. 'Poor Darren, he couldn't do right for wrong in my eyes and his tensions were probably high as well,' she recalls regretfully.

By now, she'd become convinced that there was something wrong with Darren and that he was suffering from birth trauma. She repeatedly told him that he was depressed and didn't know how to deal with the birth. 'It was just easier for me to think, "It's not me, it's Darren."'

Darren went along with it because he was worried about how she'd react if he refused to go. As he left, Danielle locked the doors of their house, pulled down the blinds and, fearing she was being spied on, unplugged the two dog cameras she'd installed to keep an eye on the dog.

Darren went to his mum's house and explained what had happened. By now, both his and Danielle's parents were seriously concerned about her state of mind.

'So when Darren said, "Dan's just kicked me out," it was the straw that broke the camel's back for his mum and mine. "Right, that's it," they said. "This can't go on."'

The mums went to speak to Danielle. 'There's something really, really wrong,' they told her.

'Oh my God, I've just got postnatal depression!' she shouted at them. 'I'm not ill, just depressed! It happens!'

When they wouldn't accept what she was saying, she became confrontational and told them to fuck off. 'And I am definitely not like that. I'm a really chilled person,' she said.

The mums went away and phoned Danielle's GP, who arranged to come to the house that evening. Meanwhile, Danielle allowed Darren to return for the night.

Darren told her that the GP was visiting him to discuss his 'depression' so that she wouldn't suspect he was coming to see her.

'Oh that's fine!' she said. 'It's great that you're getting help.'

When the GP arrived that night at ten, Danielle told him her entire birth story in lengthy detail while he tried to assess her mental state. And, although the GP agreed with Darren that something wasn't right with her, he didn't see her as a threat to herself or her child at that point. He told Darren that he couldn't have her sectioned. Instead, he made arrangements for her to go to the local hospital the next day.

Early the next morning, Danielle's whole family arrived at the house. 'How do you fancy having a trip up to the hospital where you had your pregnancy scans?' her mum said. 'Wouldn't it be lovely to have a walk round the hospital with your new baby?'

Since it wasn't the hospital where she had given birth, this seemed like a good idea to Danielle.

At the hospital, her mum and Darren led her to the psychiatric unit, where a couple of staff assessed her in a side room.

'Automatically, I felt threatened and intimidated and kept asking why they wanted to know all of these things,' she remembered. 'Eventually, it got to a point where they showed me a consent form and asked me to read my name and address in the top left-hand corner. What's bizarre is that the words were all back to front; they looked like Egyptian hieroglyphics. I couldn't read my own name.'

By the time she was admitted to the unit and given a tour of the facilities, around midday, she had lost all knowledge of having a baby and thought she was a new member of staff being shown around her ward. She had no idea she was being admitted as an inpatient. But as the hours passed and none of the staff responded to her as colleagues normally would, she realised that she wasn't working there. Instead, she was taking part in a reality show, she decided.

'I started to run around the unit – I was manic and so delusional that I thought I was in a game and the aim of the game was to find the exit to this place I was in.'

When the unit staff tried to give her a medication that she hadn't heard of, she refused to take it.

She became convinced that she had to find and solve clues that would lead her to being able to unlock the door to the ward's phone cubicle, where she would be able to phone her mum and say, 'I've won the challenge and I'm ready to come home!'

She went round the ward asking the other inpatients questions that would help her solve the challenge. If any of them had a name that remotely sounded like the name of somebody she knew, in her mind, they became that person. Whenever she heard the sound of voices, she thought she could hear members of her family talking about her.

'I thought my family were all behind screens watching me and conversing about how I was getting on in this big game show. But as the night went on, I thought, "Wow, this game is a lot harder than I thought it was."

'I went on the defensive and started shouting at people. I shouted at this poor healthcare assistant. I ran around setting off fire alarms and pressing buzzers, doing whatever I could to just get some attention, I guess, because I just didn't know what was going on.'

At five to eleven that night, she got into a confrontation with staff about leaving the communal telly room because she was convinced that her family were coming to pick her up at eleven o'clock.

'No one's coming to pick you up, lovely,' the staff said.

'Yes, they are!' she insisted.

The confrontation got out of hand and she was given an injection of something to calm her down. 'I imagine it was diazepam but I still don't know to this day,' she said.

She slept for six hours. Her mum and Darren visited her in the unit the next morning.

'They begged, "If you love April and you love Darren, please take this medication,"' she recalled, 'and something just clicked. I thought, "Of course I love my family and they want the best for me."'

She took the medication, which was an antipsychotic drug, and slept for nearly 24 hours, catching up on the sleep she'd missed in the previous two weeks. When she woke up, she was completely disorientated. 'Why am I here?' she thought.

She went down to the nurses' station and said to one of the nurses, 'Can you help me? I don't know what's going on.'

'It's nice to see you again. Here's some information for you,' he said.

He gave her a leaflet on postpartum psychosis and, as she read it through, back in her room, 'It was like a brick had landed on my lap,' she said. 'I thought, "As a midwife, you might go your whole career without meeting anyone who has postpartum psychosis – and it happened to me!" It was such a surreal moment.'

She walked back to the nurses' station and was given permission to call her mum.

She could hear the relief in her mum's voice as she spoke to her. 'It's lovely that you're back!' her mum said. 'You're doing great!' They had a giggle and a bit of a cry together on the phone.

The antipsychotic medicine worked remarkably quickly and Danielle was allowed day release on her fourth day in the unit. She was then offered a place in a mother and baby unit two and a half hours from home.

'I knew from my work that places in a mother and baby unit are very sought after. We definitely need more of them because it's not acceptable to expect your family to get in a car and travel two and a half hours to see you and then two and a half hours back again. But I felt I had no choice but to accept the place because if I stayed in the unit, I couldn't be with my daughter.'

During my time filming at Springfield hospital, I met people who absconded while on day release if the unit was too far away from their family. It's where it's placed geographically that often determines how people behave in that situation and can affect their chances of recovery. Distance also has a financial impact. Darren and Danielle had put aside savings for having a baby but most of it went on B&Bs for Darren when he came to visit Danielle and April in the mother and baby unit.

As I've never visited a mother and baby unit, I was curious to know what it was like there and whether the staff were very hands on. 'They were very friendly and helpful,' Danielle said. 'I didn't need any practical help, even though they offered it, but you could walk up to any one of them and they would sit with you and chat with you, which was great. They are crucially important for mums getting over postnatal illness, which is why I'm now working alongside Swansea Trust to try to get a mother and baby unit here in Wales.'

I wondered how she got on with the other inpatients. 'What I found interesting was that we were all professional women in high-pressure jobs,' Danielle said. 'There was me, a midwife; there was a psychiatric nurse, a teacher and a lawyer. We all connected and I still speak to them today.'

Danielle went home after ten days and had regular visits from a community nurse to check up on her. As she recovered, she began to process what had happened and was hit by guilt and grief as she mourned the loss of those early precious days with a new baby. 'As I tumbled down into depression, I thought, "Am I feeling this way because of what I've gone through? Or would I have felt it anyway?"'

For Danielle, having PND and knowing she was depressed but not being able to do anything about it was worse than being psychotic. 'You don't know that you're psychotic but you know that you've got postnatal depression because you wake up every morning with that horrible anxiety in your belly. I couldn't get rid of it. I kept crying to the nurse and saying, "I'm so miserable!"'

It took eight months for her to regain her confidence and stop worrying that she wasn't a good enough mum. 'What got me better? I joined lots of mum and baby groups, which was lovely and kept my mind active while Darren was at work.'

Understandably, she felt nervous about telling other mums about what had happened to her. 'I wanted them to know why I wasn't myself but I couldn't just say, "You'll never guess what happened!" and have a chat about it over coffee. It was such a weird thing.'

None of her friends, when she told them, had heard of postpartum psychosis. 'I really had to go into detail and explain that it is a recognised thing. The work that I do now is about helping other women who go through it because I don't want anyone ever to feel the way I felt when I came home with that realisation: oh God, this happened to me!'

I was very grateful to Danielle for telling me her story so selflessly and I was delighted to see her so well because when we were filming on the psychosis ward at Springfield it was hard to imagine some of the inpatients making a full recovery. The experts were telling me, 'You're seeing this patient and it's breaking your heart because she hasn't got a clue what day it is but if you see her in 12 or 18 months' time, she'll probably be back at work.'

That's why Danielle was so inspiring.

'I went back to work after nine months,' she said. 'I could have had a year off work if I'd wanted to but I needed to gain a sense of who I was again. I wasn't just a mum that this had happened to and my life wasn't washing bottles and weaning. I was a professional person and I had to go back and do something, just for a day – just for a 12-hour shift – where I could be me again. Over time, that really helped me access who I was before I had a child.

'I love being a mum. It's the best thing in the world but it's not all I am and I think it's really important to remember that.'

6

Anti-LGBTQ+ Abuse and Discrimination

Ellis, Harry, Blue, Evelyn, Jessica and 2BU

When I was planning this book, I felt it was my responsibility to speak to communities that I'm not necessarily a part of day-to-day – and that included the LGBTQ+ community. Lots of my LGBTQ+ pals have said they've been up against it at times in terms of their mental health and I wanted to learn more. Thankfully, we've come a long way since 1952, when the American Psychiatric Association included homosexuality in its *Diagnostic and Statistical Manual of Mental Disorders* (*DSM-I*) and a number of people were put through painful and damaging 'treatment' to try to 'cure' them of their completely normal feelings. Homosexuality was decriminalised in the UK in 1967 (this still throws me that it wasn't actually that long ago) and removed from *DSM-III* in 1973; same-sex marriage is now recognised and many people in prominent public life are gay or trans and, quite rightly, proud of who they are.

So I guess you could argue that on the surface, things are so much better than they used to be.

That's not to say, however, that there isn't a disproportionate instance of mental health issues in the LGBTQ+ community, or that each of the groups within that community doesn't have its own specific dynamics and challenges. But there is increasing evidence that experiencing anti-LGBTQ+ abuse and discrimination on the street, at home and at work significantly increases the risk of poor mental health, and my understanding is that some of my friends have experienced certain mental health issues because of how they've been treated. Some people have behaved towards them in an entirely different way from my non-LGBTQ+ friends, and it's understandably had a knock-on effect.

According to Rethink Mental Illness, research shows that LGBTQ+ people are one and a half times more likely to develop depression and anxiety compared to the rest of the population. And when you read government data that shows that in the year to March 2020 in England and Wales, reported sexual orientation hate crimes rose by 19 per cent and transgender identity hate crimes by 16 per cent, averaging more than 50 reports of hate crimes against the LGBTQ+ community each day (and it's estimated that four out of five incidents go unreported), you can't help thinking that experiencing stigma and prejudice is a contributing factor to LGBTQ+ mental health figures.

Reading the stats and listening to my pals made me want to hear what LGBTQ+ youngsters have to say on the subject, which is how I came to meet Ellis, a bright, engaging 20-year-old science student, just as his term at uni was winding down.

Ellis was a total sweetheart. He was concerned that his experiences weren't extreme enough to include in a book about mental health but when he spoke to me over Zoom from his bedroom at college he admitted to feeling very anxious about going home for the Christmas holidays. Being at home with his parents is always difficult for him, he explained, because although they know he is gay, they don't approve. They don't make it obvious but they never refer to his sexuality, so there's this big unspoken 'thing' when he's at home and he can't be himself, which is a constant strain.

Ellis remembers experiencing discrimination for the first time when he was at school, aged 12, but he'd first sensed he was gay at the age of 10 or 11, he told me. 'I didn't know what it was exactly – I just knew it was something. I think a lot of people say the same thing.'

When you're that age, you so desperately want to fit in, so, like his mates, he started going out with girls. 'I used that as sort of a defence mechanism when people at school mentioned that I had a high-pitched voice or was quite camp. "No, I have a girlfriend," I'd say.'

Studies show that in 2012, when Ellis was at school, 55 per cent of LGBTQ+ school pupils experienced bullying because of their sexual orientation. Just horrifying.

'I guess that was the first time I started to realise that something was "different" because people were making comments,' Ellis said. 'I was lucky that I found a way to deflect them but repressing it definitely had an impact.'

Over the next year, Ellis became quite depressed and started to self-harm. 'I didn't really know what was wrong or why I was feeling down but there was a background feeling of maybe this isn't right. Maybe the feelings I'm having shouldn't be there.'

He thought he knew what his parents would think if he expressed his feelings – his dad would roll his eyes and tut if he saw someone flamboyantly gay in the street – so there seemed to be no one around to talk to. He used self-harming as a way of venting his frustration, he said, like punching a wall. He had no idea that other people did it too, until eventually he confided in a friend at school who was also self-harming and they managed to pull each other out of it.

A little later, Ellis came out as bisexual to his close friends, as a 'stepping stone' to feeling more comfortable with his sexual orientation. Still, there was uncertainty. It wasn't until he watched a coming-out video on YouTube that he felt validated and more grounded in his feelings. (Coming-out videos often feature people talking about their coming-out experiences or show them actually coming out to family members or friends.) Going out with a boy was the next step; he met someone at a concert when he was 15 and they started a relationship – but this wasn't easy either. Even a simple thing like meeting up in Manchester and going to the cinema was fraught with worry.

'We were always out in town because I couldn't tell my parents and he couldn't tell his, and I felt very self-conscious of people seeing us and looking at us. They probably weren't but in my head that's what was happening and it wore me down.'

Every time he thought about coming out to his parents, he considered the possibility that he'd be kicked out of home and never see them again. Then, about two months after he met his boyfriend, his parents confronted him.

'Have you got something to tell us?' they asked.

'No,' he said.

He didn't realise that they'd been snooping through his phone and seen all his texts to his boyfriend. It was a tough moment because he was only just building up to feeling comfortable with telling people he was gay.

When he acknowledged the truth to his parents, there wasn't an argument. 'It was more disappointment,' he recalled. 'My mum was crying and my dad, who's quite old and more traditional, sat there, stone-faced, and looked at the wall.'

They didn't kick him out, either. He went to stay with a friend that night and, when he came back the next day, they acted as if nothing had happened.

'We never spoke about it again – and never have,' Ellis said. 'It was never mentioned.'

Since he hadn't been accepted or entirely rejected, he entered a kind of limbo. There was a lot of tension in the house after that and an underlying hostility coming from his parents.

'We didn't speak to each other properly for about a year,' he said. 'It was just smalltalk, like, "What's for tea?" or stuff about school. It was horrible not talking about it.

'In some ways, I'd rather have been told, "No, we don't accept this. Leave," because then I'd have known where I stood. Or, if they'd acted unreasonably or had an angry reaction, I would have left home. The uncertainty was the worst part of it. All the work I'd done to make myself feel better came crashing down.'

Going along with the pretence that nothing had changed made him depressed again. 'I had this weight on me at all times; I could never catch a break. I felt constantly drained because I had to be on guard and watch what I said and did. Even to this day, I struggle to relax properly.'

He didn't tell anyone how he was feeling. He self-harmed again a handful of times but realised that it wasn't a healthy coping mechanism and instead focused on his schoolwork, using it as a way to distract himself from the underlying pain of never talking about being gay with his mum and dad.

He couldn't find any advice online. 'I don't think there's enough support for that specific situation: where you're still living at home and everyone knows but it's not open, it's not "a good thing" and it's not talked about. I think it's much more common than people think.'

His hard work at school paid off and he was the first of his family to go to uni. His parents were incredibly proud, which helped repair their relationship, but still nothing was ever said about him being gay.

It was so ingrained in Ellis to behave in a 'not gay' way at home that it wasn't until he moved out that he realised how guarded he'd been. But at uni, he has found a safe space to be his authentic self.

'Even simple things, like when I'm cooking, I put stupid music on and dance around the kitchen. I would never do that at home, where I would always be sombre and calm, so as not to aggravate things.'

He now has a boyfriend whose parents are fully accepting and this sometimes saddens Ellis. 'We'll be in bed watching a movie and his parents will call and I'll talk to them, and it hurts in the sense that I know my parents will never do that. Even in 20 years' time, I know it will never get to that level of acceptance. It's difficult to deal with: my boyfriend is a big part of my life and my happiness and yet I can't introduce him to my family.'

The hostility at home has ebbed but Ellis isn't sure whether this is because he's more confident in himself or because his parents are less uncomfortable with him being gay. They still haven't said anything relating to his sexual orientation but he always senses it there in the background. So he lives two separate lives and tries not to think about it too much – because that's his best way to cope at the moment.

One comfort is the presence at home of his 12-year-old brother, who isn't bothered and appears, thankfully, more accepting.

'I came out to him before I went to uni and his reaction really helped me,' Ellis told me. 'He looked up from his video game, said, "Oh, it's OK. I still love you," and carried on playing. It didn't faze him at all, which was such a shock to me. We've grown up in the same household but he's got a completely different attitude because he's learnt about LGBT issues at school in PSHE.'

It's cheering that education seems to be changing the climate but it's clear that there's still a long way to go. A 2017 report commissioned by Stonewall with the Centre for Family Research at the University of Cambridge into the experiences of over 3,700 lesbian, gay, bi and trans pupils in Britain's schools found that although attitudes have improved since 2012, almost half of all LGBTQ+ pupils still face bullying at school.

For young people in the community who are transgender and non-binary, finding acceptance appears especially tough. This was obvious when I spoke to Harry, a very sweet young man of 23 who was born female. Harry is an MA student applying for jobs in renewable energy but when he spoke to me from his family home in Cornwall, he explained he was finding it hard having to explain and justify himself every time he went for a job interview.

'I've only been on hormones for a few months and don't necessarily get seen as a man,' he told me. 'So I have to come out every single time I'm introduced to anyone new and I have anxiety about how that person is going to react. No one has been abusive but people have said things like, "OK, I'll call you Harry but you're always going to be a woman." You hear that so often and you can't argue back because you're worried they'll get violent or angry.'

I asked him why he thought people are so hesitant to treat people how they deserve to be treated.

'It's a hard topic to understand,' he said. 'If you haven't lived with gender dysphoria, you can't imagine thinking of yourself as the opposite gender.' (Gender dysphoria is the unhappiness a person can feel about the mismatch between their gender identity – or personal feelings about their gender – and their sex assigned at birth.)

'And people are a little bit afraid of what they can't wrap their head around, and some react to that with anger,' Harry continued. It was a generous way to look at it and obviously something he'd thought about a lot. 'It still sucks, though,' he added.

Harry first realised he was Harry when he was 13 and discovered that a person could be transgender. 'Growing up, I always knew that something was missing. I almost felt like an outcast before I knew I was trans. Then, as soon as I found out that transgender was a thing, the pieces fell into place.'

But it was five years before he felt ready to come out to his family, even though he was pretty sure they would be supportive. No matter how accepting your parents are, he explained, every LGBTQ+ teenager has to consider the idea that if they come out, they might get rejected because who they are might be some kind of disqualifier from being part of their family.

Lisa, CEO and youth worker at 2BU, a youth support group for LGBTQ+ young people in Somerset, explained to me why coming out can be a particular challenge for transgender people: 'One of our young people said something huge to me years ago,' she said. 'They said, "When you come out as gay to a person, you're giving them a piece of information that they can just put in their pocket and know about you. But if you come out as transgender to them, you're really asking them to make changes. You want them to change how they see you, what they call you, how they refer to you and all of the things that they need to do for you. It's not information that they can just put away; you're asking them to really know it."'

Wrapped up in the idea that coming out to his folks wouldn't go well, Harry became depressed. It felt like a huge weight to be keeping such a massive secret – it meant that, even though he was close to his family and friends, no one knew who he really was. 'I just don't think any teenager should have to bear that,' he said.

I asked him how it felt to be depressed. 'People think it means you're sad all the time,' he told me, 'but actually you don't feel anything. You wake up, go through the motions and that's it. There's no big sadness or big happiness. It's the same thing every single day; you just feel numb.'

Five years is a very long time to be living with depression, especially when you're a teen. 'How do you feel about life before you were who you are?' I asked him.

'It's like I was playing a character, like the old me was someone I was acting for 18 years,' he said.

Harry went off to uni on the other side of the country and, shortly afterwards, wrote to his mum, explaining that he was trans. His letter was full of apologies and a plea for acceptance. The next two days were the most nerve racking of his life but fortunately his mum's response was positive.

'I was very, very lucky, in that my parents said, "Great. A hundred per cent." They were super-supportive and said they had always known it was coming.'

He began to recover from depression and described his recovery as, 'One of the best feelings you'll ever feel. It's like falling in love with everything. If you're in a car, listening to music, you think, "Yeah, this is great!" You feel everything intensely because you're so used to not feeling it.'

But he still has to negotiate the relationship between accepting who he is and getting others to accept who he is. I wondered how taxing that's been on his mental health?

'I think the biggest thing has been the anxiety,' he said. 'It's a huge weight off your shoulders to be out. You're happy every day. But the anxiety is always there, in every little thing, every single time I leave the house, and it gets overwhelming at times.'

Just everyday encounters with strangers – for instance, when Harry goes to the shops, he worries about which changing room he'll be directed to. It may sound like a small thing to some but he doesn't feel confident enough to argue about going to the men's and he doesn't want to go to the women's.

I cannot imagine, I told him. I really cannot imagine, as a straight cis woman, how it feels to leave your front door, thinking, 'Am I going to get hassle today? Am I going to meet people who will have prejudices about me? Who will flat out refuse to accept me? Or think they know more about me than I do … ?'

On a more personal level, every time one of his pals gets a girlfriend or boyfriend and introduces them to Harry, he thinks, 'This person could hate who I am – and I have to be prepared for that.'

'Every single new person I meet is someone who could potentially be hateful,' he said.

A lot of Harry's fears stem from what he sees and reads on social media. 'Any time there's an article about trans people or gay people, you see a lot of nasty comments – and the people writing those comments exist in real life. So every single time you meet someone new, you're worried they might be one of them. It creates this anxiety that you just never shake.'

At the place where he currently works to fund his studies, some of Harry's colleagues added him on social media and appeared to accept him for who he is, but then he saw them making anti-trans comments on other posts. 'They're alright to me face-to-face and then I'm watching them online be not OK with me,' he told me ruefully.

He feels nervous a lot of the time, which is exhausting, and he has insomnia as well. 'My anxiety gets really bad at night. I lie awake and think, "I'm not going to find a job. I'm not going to find a flat. What if the landlord doesn't like trans people?" You go over and over it in your head.'

A lot of his worry is focused on forging a career because he's going into an industry where people tend to be 'traditional' and older. And, as it is for so many trans people, his physical transition is going painfully slowly.

He waited more than two and a half years before he could even start the process. 'You need to see two doctors and you can't start hormones until you've seen the second doctor and been diagnosed,' he explained. 'You have to meet their criteria, so you're incredibly nervous that you're going to say something wrong and they'll decide you're faking it.'

There will be individuals who will say, 'You have to take your time,' because in some instances, people have changed their mind. I accept that we have to acknowledge that but we also must acknowledge that there are so many people who are not able to live their true authentic lives. It feels cruel to be forcing Harry and other people to wait years just to simply be themselves.

Harry agrees that we need the assessment process so that people can make sure it's a hundred per cent the right thing to do. 'But I don't think anyone should be waiting two years for what is essentially a life-saving treatment,' he said.

A survey published midway through 2021 showed that LGBTQ+ young people are three times more likely to self-harm and twice as likely to contemplate suicide as their non-LGBTQ+ peers. The research was carried out by the young people's charity Just Like Us, who surveyed nearly 3,000 pupils aged 11–18 between December 2020 and January 2021.

I asked Harry if he'd ever thought not being here would be better than being here?

'When I came out, I was at a crossroads: either I come out now or I don't make it to my nineteenth birthday,' he said. 'I made the choice to come out but some people make the other one.'

It's heartbreaking to think how close to the edge he was. I wondered what message he would like to put out there when it comes to transgender rights and mental health.

'That the easiest thing in the world is to call someone by their right name and you can save lives doing it,' he said, without hesitation. 'When someone calls me Harry, it makes my day better, it genuinely does, even this many years down the line. So I just don't understand why you wouldn't do it.'

In an ideal world, he'd like to be able to say, 'This is who I am,' and for the response to be accepting.

Not having to constantly justify himself – just acceptance. Genuine acceptance.

'I'm constantly told, "People don't have to accept you if they don't want to," and I say, "But they do. Because I'm here. I'm not asking them to throw me a party, just to use the right name for me and the right pronouns, and not to be harsh online to kids who are just trying to find themselves." If you accept trans people, you're probably saving lives.'

I really liked Harry. I was so grateful to him for speaking to me and in my subsequent conversations with trans people I heard again and again that being called by the correct name and pronouns is a vital part of feeling accepted.

Twenty-two year-old Blue, who is non-binary and uses the pronouns they/their, prepared a PowerPoint presentation for their mother to explain the situation, which was taking things to a level of organisation I aspire to (but don't often manage to achieve … OK, never manage!). I asked Blue if they would be willing to explain to me in layperson's terms what it means to be non-binary, even though it's a question that's been put to them so many times before.

'For me, it's not liking the idea of being perceived as a man or as a woman, and wanting to exist outside of and in between that,' they said.

Blue is often asked why they are non-binary and I just can't imagine how exhausting it must be having to explain yourself so often. (The irony that I was indeed also asking questions was not lost on me … So I checked that they were genuinely happy to contribute to this conversation!) For Blue and Harry and other trans and non-binary people, I guess that every time you interact with someone new, you think, 'Here we go, again, I've got justify myself.'

So Blue's PowerPoint actually sounds like a really useful thing to do because I think that, sometimes, when people make mistakes in their conversations with LGBTQ+ people, it's not always out of malice or spite. I don't think people always intend to be cruel (or maybe I'm just being too optimistic!). It's that they just don't know or haven't read enough, or they're not up to speed and they don't hang out with people who aren't exactly the same as them, and, as a result, their language can feel a bit ignorant or awkward or clumsy, and the people they're talking to can, quite rightly, feel offended.

'There is a problem with people not understanding the gravity of the situation or just being ignorant,' Blue said. 'But you never have to worry if all you have is good intent,' they added. 'The amount of times that someone has to come out is infinite, so they're going to be tired but they're also going to be used to it and it's very unlikely that anyone's going to get really angry at you if you just slip up and make a mistake.'

If you feel unsure, don't be afraid to ask, they added. 'You could ask, "Hey, what are your pronouns? What's the name that you want to be used for you? And is it OK to use that name and those pronouns in front of these people?" So as long as you're open and willing to be educated and talk about it, but also conscious of the fact that you don't want to overwhelm someone who's queer with intrusive questions, you'll be fine.'

I personally found this advice super useful! I always really want to make people feel respected and comfy, but I also accept I don't know everything, in terms of thoughtful language and what could be triggering, and so I always want to check what I'm saying is appropriate. I'd be devastated if I upset someone. So, I basically try to have as many conversations as possible and continue to try and educate myself, without being too 'grabby'.

Of the PowerPoint, Blue said, 'I just wanted to explain it all to my mum in depth. So the first slide was, "Here is what bisexuality is." At the time, I identified as genderqueer or genderfluid, so the next slide was, "Here's what that means. And here's what it means to me. There you go."'

(There's a lot of discussion about the differences between the terms non-binary, genderqueer and genderfluid, but there seems to be some consensus that non-binary is a descriptive term; genderqueer has a similar meaning but is open to a more personal, individual interpretation; and genderfluid describes shifting identity, or gender questioning. Gender can definitely be a journey and Blue now identifies as non-binary and trans.)

Blue wasn't happy at the end of the PowerPoint when their mum said, 'I don't see why you have to tell me this.'

But although they felt upset at the time, they've since realised that their mum meant well. 'I think what she meant was, "It's not a big deal. You're you and I love you." She just went around the wrong way,' Blue said. 'It was as if in her mind, being queer was just normal: she didn't have to think about it; she didn't see why I had to think about it. But it was really important for me.

'She also said, "Whatever you do, don't change your body and don't change how you are or how you look," when I talked about being genderqueer. That's not what you want to hear! But she was accepting, mainly, and said, "I just love you and I'm pleased to see you out if you want to be."'

I wondered whether Blue thought that, as a society, although we've now thankfully understood that some people are born in the wrong body, we're not quite there when it comes to genderfluid, for example, or non-binary?

'Do you feel like some people want you to pick a side?' I asked. 'Like they're saying, "Who are you? Are you male or female? Why can't you put yourself in one of two camps?"'

Clearly, Blue knows a lot more about it than I do but I think that on the whole we're kind of desperate to put people in their box and label them, so that we can understand them. 'Is this our next hurdle when it comes to educating ourselves?' I wondered.

'I think people definitely understand the binary a lot more,' Blue agreed. 'They say, "Oh, OK. You want to switch from this to this?" That's how they're thinking about it. But I sit in the middle, saying, "What's my gender? No, I don't have one. Leave me out of it." And they're like, "Oh, but what bathroom do you go in? What are you going to wear if you've got no gender? Where do you shop?" I'm like, "Well, you've created this world for me, where you say I have to pick one gender. But I don't want either, I want both." And often people say, "That doesn't exist. It can't happen."'

A few years ago, Blue's mum commented on how young people 'keep coming up with new labels and inventing new identities for themselves'. She understands more now but Blue thinks that a lot of people are puzzled in the way their mum was.

'They think we're just "coming up with things" when really this has existed for so long but there were no words for it. We're now just articulating it. Accepting ideas like non-binary and different non-traditional relationships is the next step but it's really hard for some people.'

'What's the relationship like between who you are, how you see yourself and how you identify?' I asked Blue. 'And what you're up against – how taxing can it be on your mental health?'

'It's a lot of anxiety,' they said. 'You're always thinking about how you're being perceived; you're thinking, "What can I say in front of this person, are they going to ask me too many questions?" You're thinking, "Is it safe for me in this area?" You're overthinking things 24/7. It's always running in your brain and taking up unnecessary space.'

I asked whether Blue's non-binary pals echoed these concerns. 'Do you think they've also had to deal with anxiety because of how society has treated them? Have other things come up in terms of mental health issues?'

'Anxiety and depression are probably at the top for trans people,' Blue replied. 'And for the trans people I know, including myself, there are a lot of body issues related to how you see yourself in the mirror and how other people see you. That can relate to genitalia, or how broad your shoulders are, or your hair, your face or weight – or all of those things.'

Blue went on to talk about how they and some of their pals bind their chest to make it flat – and some people bind it for too long, even though it can be painful, or harmful. 'You can't fathom taking it off and then it takes a toll on your brain because maybe the next day you realise you're a bit sore and can't wear it again, and then you feel awful that day because you feel bad in your body ...'

Gender dysphoria often has an impact on mental health for these kinds of reasons, Blue explained. Unfortunately, many LGBTQ+ people fear facing discrimination and unfair treatment when accessing healthcare services, including for mental health issues, and so often don't seek or get help when they experience difficulties. According to a 2018 Stonewall report on LGBT health, one in four patients had witnessed negative remarks about LGBT people from healthcare staff while accessing services. One in seven LGBT people said they had avoided treatment altogether for fear of the discrimination they may face.

'But we shouldn't have to be too scared to talk to people,' Blue said.

Blue remembers having an argument on Twitter a few years back, after they posted that they believed gender doesn't exist. 'In that case, how can trans people exist?' argued another Twitter user.

'You're right!' Blue agreed. 'Also you're wrong, although I can't explain why.'

'People are saying, "This is what a man looks like; this is what a female looks like," and trans people are thinking, "I don't look like that. I don't like that. I don't want to be that." But if we didn't have gender, no one would be saying, "This is how you're supposed to look," so it wouldn't be a problem.'

I wondered whether Blue thought that the current widespread perception of gender doesn't work for anyone?

'There are women who don't feel feminine enough; they are seeking an ideal of how they should be because of gender,' Blue said. 'And there are men who think, "This is how I should be and this is how I should act," and it ends up as toxic masculinity. That's all because we have this gender binary and this gender construct that's imprinted on us, which is really frustrating. Because if we didn't have it, then people could just be and exist; if we didn't have it, people would just be people.'

What Blue said got me thinking about the women I know who love being women, who enjoy putting on high heels and dressing up. I once met a Russian sex worker who oozed traditional femininity and revelled in being adored by men. You could speculate and ask how much of that was sincere, but actually I think it was.

I asked Blue whether they ever met resistance from women who say, 'Actually, I really enjoy being a woman. And I truly feel like a woman. And it's really important to me that I'm able to keep hold of that.'

'Sometimes people do have that mentality,' Blue said. 'They say, "I'm so proud to be a woman," which they absolutely should be.'

Blue has no argument with that. 'But when they say, "I'm proud to be a woman and you should be proud to be a woman, too," and I say, "But I'm not," and they say, "That's because you're not proud," I'm like, "Argh!"'

I can imagine it would be very frustrating. It sounds really cheesy and such a cliché but I have nothing but admiration for people who are courageous enough to be themselves, because it's not easy. That's what my trans pals say: 'No one would choose this because it's such a saga. This isn't a choice, it's who we are. No one wants to make life unnecessarily difficult for themselves.'

While I was researching this chapter, I was given the chance to sit in on a chat with some of the members of 2BU, the youth support and awareness-raising group for LGBTQ+ people in Somerset. There were about 15 trans and non-binary people in the chatroom and everybody was so honest and candid that it was a really remarkable meeting. I felt privileged to be invited into such a caring and nurturing environment.

During our hour-long chat, the 2BU group talked over a wide range of topics: anxiety, depression, suicidal thoughts, gender dysphoria, coming out, discrimination, bullying and education.

'The LGBT community (especially the youth) has a bit of a running joke,' said Theo, a member of the group who identifies as non-binary, 'and it's essentially that when gay people meet, we skip the casual coffee days and playing games and go straight to the deep emotional things.'

That nailed it. It was great that humour was never far from the surface but the issues being discussed at the meeting were deadly serious. It struck me that these were young people who just wanted to be themselves and explore who they were becoming, and yet from what they were saying, you could tell that life rarely felt carefree.

Before we started, we introduced ourselves with our pronouns, which I'd never done before. 'Hi, I'm Stacey and I use the pronouns she/her,' I said.

'Folk often get misgendered,' said Lisa, who runs 2BU. 'We often get read by people and this can be based on their own experiences or assumptions according to, perhaps, appearances or a person's name. So what we're saying is, "We share our own pronouns as an indication of how we would like to be referred to in the third person. Sharing our own pronouns promotes an actively inclusive environment and by using someone's shared pronouns we know this is hugely validating, and demonstrates our care and respect for them."'

When I asked the group if they'd be willing to talk about what's hardest about being part of the trans community, several of them mentioned being called by the wrong pronouns. 'I have never been rightly gendered by a stranger, which very much sucks,' said Nathaniel, a trans man.

Nathaniel had to come out three times to his family before they finally took him seriously. Now, after having been perceived as female for 16 years, he was feeling grief for the childhood he had missed. 'Tiny things, like having space bedsheets or playing with Nerf guns – and I would have loved going to boys' birthday parties,' he said. 'I missed out on those little rites of passages and I'm never going to have them now, which brings a big sense of loss for me.'

But Nathaniel was also ready with an answer when I asked what was joyous about being part of the trans community: 'It's being able to construct yourself, I think: you're kind of starting anew and you don't have as much of a base to start on, so you can really choose who you want to be. I like that. It's very freeing for me.'

This seemed to suggest that he'd be hopeful of enjoying things in the future.

'This community is very supportive of mental health,' said Theo, 'and I have never been so supported or had a group of people that I would more consider family than 2BU.'

Like Nathaniel, Theo also had to look outside their family and home to find acceptance and a place where they didn't feel judged.

'I've been out for two and a half years now, to my folks, and my mum has just started trying to use my name,' Theo said. 'The other day, she said, "I used to hate the fact that you were trans. I don't hate it anymore." And that's as far as we've gotten in two and a half years! My dad and my step-mum still don't use my name. Nor do my brother or my stepsister. When I tried to correct my stepsister, she said, "Well, the last time I checked, you had this and that part of your body ..."'

For Christmas, Theo was planning to give their parents a book about parenting a transgender child, which seems like a great idea if it helps them to understand what's going on with them.

Several members of the group said that being 'dead-named' – being called by the name you had before you came out as trans – could be very hurtful, especially when done deliberately.

Kip, a trans lad, recalled being misgendered by a friend he'd grown up with. 'We were very close and I came out to her as trans. She was very dismissive of it. She said, "Yeah, OK," but then didn't make any effort to use my name or pronouns and admitted that she also had another non-binary friend who she also constantly misgendered. I have tried so many times to get her to understand that this is very important to me.'

It's one thing if strangers don't accept you, or if they judge you, but I can't imagine how tricky it must be when it's coming from someone you really love and rate because all you're asking is for them to love you – your authentic self.

'When people you're close to don't make any moves to try to help out and do the small things, you come to a point where you think, "OK, they love the person that they wish I was, not the person I am," Theo said.

This brought to mind something that Harry had said: it might take a while to get used to switching someone's pronouns but just trying is easy. You'd at least try, wouldn't you, if you loved someone?

I asked the group how it felt to have your existence or identity constantly questioned.

'It feels like I'm being treated as lower than what I am at a base level, which is a human being,' said Evelyn, an 18-year-old trans woman. 'It feels like I'm being singled out from everyone else for doing something as simple as going outside of the cis-het normality and expressing who I am as a person. It shouldn't be happening.'

Evelyn said that one of the huge challenges of being part of the LGBTQ+ community is the number of people she meets or is in contact with who are struggling with mental health issues, including suicidal thoughts and attempts. In fact, several of the group spoke about how they'd had to talk people down from suicide threats, call an ambulance for someone who had made an attempt or stay on the phone until a distressed friend had finally fallen asleep.

As Lisa, the group youth worker said, 'For all of us here in the room, we're looking after our own mental health and also supporting other LGBTQ+ people that we know around us. This emotional labour can feel like a huge burden:

one, we're educating the universe; two, we're looking after ourselves and three, we're looking after our peers.'

Sometimes these young people seemed far older than their years, including Byron, a trans man who talked about the impact of not feeling accepted. Noting that suicide and self-harm are extremely prevalent in the community, he said that many cases go unreported because people keep them quiet.

'Over the span of 2015 to 2016, which was when I was coming to terms with my gender, I attempted 12 times,' Byron said. 'The last time was in 2016, when my mum basically said, when I came out to her, "No, you're not trans."'

Byron's mum is now much more accepting of him, which is something to feel hopeful about. 'It just took a lot of time – and to be met with just NO was hard to hear. Mental health becomes an extreme struggle if you're just told no, you can't be yourself. There will be attempts, there will be self-harm and there is a lot of homelessness.'

Theo felt that not being open when they were younger had a knock-on effect when it came to their mental health. 'I grew up hiding parts of myself that my parents and the people around me didn't like and it became second nature to hide everything. I think that when you grow up hiding parts of yourself, you end up hiding everything, so when my mental health started declining, it was second nature to hide it – I didn't even think about telling anyone else because I just never had.'

'Are we making progress as a society?' I asked the group. 'Do you feel hopeful?'

'I think that the country is making progress,' Evelyn said, 'but there is still a large amount of pushback from the community, especially from parents, about LGBTQ+ education in schools, which is an integral part of reducing discrimination: talking about it and understanding it. I am, however, cautiously hopeful that through activism, public pressure and organised efforts, among other methods, we as a community will break through to a better tomorrow for everyone, not just us.'

'What needs to change?' I asked. 'What would you like to see happen?'

'I think education needs to be standardised, or at least organised, for LGBTQ+ issues. There also needs to be harsher scrutiny and potentially harsher punishments for hate speech, and I would like to see members of the government actively combating these issues rather than offering token words of support and empty gestures. The Equality Act was a good start and offers a great baseline but it is by no means the solution for something that has been a problem for decades, if not centuries.'

I wondered whether anyone felt that attitudes in schools had improved.

'I get really nervous about going to school because I'm scared what people think of me,' Kai said. 'Most people at my school know who I used to be, which makes it harder for me to deal with it. It does bring me down a lot and sometimes I have no idea what to do.'

'A big part of our problems isn't just within us,' Nathaniel added. 'It's because the world in many ways is not built for us and some people just don't want us around.'

'At school, when I'm walking with my boyfriend,' Kai went on, 'we get water bottles, cans, pens and things like that thrown at us. I sometimes get called slurs by kids in my year group. There was this time I was walking from performing arts (I'm dropping this subject soon because of things like this) and a group of girls followed me to where my mum now picks me up. They kept pulling my bag and my hair and saying, "Wait until tomorrow. We can't promise you'll still be in one piece." My friends and bystanders in my year were trying to stop them but they wouldn't stop. I didn't go to school for a few days after that because both me, my mum and my friends were scared of what else would happen to me.'

School should be a haven, a place of safety, so it's worrying to hear stories like this. Fortunately, Kai has also had positive experiences at his school. 'My performing arts teacher had no idea I'm trans. I was in a lot of pain the other day and she let me sit out. I then came out to her and she was like, "Oh I had no idea. Are you on testosterone yet or do you just have a deep voice?"'

When Kai told his teacher that he was too young to start hormone treatment, she said she was proud of him for coming out to her. It's great to think that at least in some schools, from some teachers, kids are getting the support they need to express themselves. We've still got a long way to go but when you think how far we've come in the last 50 years, there's hope that we're still moving towards a place of greater tolerance, acceptance and understanding.

I was reminded of how things used to be when I worked with Jessica, a beautiful, outgoing trans woman in her thirties, on a programme I presented in 2020. Jessica is fantastic: bright, strong and determined. She really has a lot going for her but when we got talking, I realised that she'd been through a lot to get to where she is now.

Jessica has a twin sister and her earliest childhood memories are of feeling confused when she was told to behave differently to her twin.

'By the age of three, it was obvious that I wasn't a typical male child,' she told me. 'Femininity just came naturally to me, it was never something that I worked towards, which is why my femininity is so authentic, because it comes from myself.'

Jessica was born in the 1980s, when the AIDS epidemic fuelled a wave of homophobia in the UK. She was teased for appearing gay and constantly asked whether she was a girl or a boy: 'So my mum would purposefully shave my hair and dress me in blue.'

Her parents divorced when she was nine and her stepfather came on the scene. 'He was very against my femininity and made it well known, so when I was 11, they sent me to an all boys school because my stepfather said they would "beat the queer out of me". That was a scary time for me. I begged and pleaded to go to a mixed school but my parents wouldn't have it, so I was lost. People at my school said, "You're different and we don't like it."'

Jessica felt a lot less loved than her twin sister and other siblings after the arrival of her stepfather, and she still feels the hurt of that unfairness. Meanwhile, at school, she found it hard to make friends because she was the subject of ridicule. 'You know what gay stands for? Got Aids Yet?' the other kids would taunt. They used to sit behind her, heat up pennies and throw them at her neck.

'I was called queer, pervert, faggot – you name it, I've been called it. I've had my head flushed down the toilet. I've been punched, I've been kicked, I've been spat on. I've been isolated. I've even been to the point of giving out sexual favours to stop people hurting me,' she recalled.

Between 1988 and 2003, section 28 of the Local Government Act 1988 prohibited 'the promotion of homosexuality' by local authorities, and it extended into schools. 'Because of section 28, no teacher was allowed to intervene to stop me having the shit kicked out of me every day at school,' Jessica told me.

It caused her a lot of anxiety, gave her a massive fear of rejection and led to long-term self-esteem issues. 'I allowed myself to be disrespected for so many years of my life to follow, in order to not be lonely or feel left out or be rejected. I even to this day allow myself to be treated less than what I am.'

When she started hormone treatment at the age of 16, her parents disowned her. Desperate for reconciliation, she allowed herself to be persuaded to stop the treatment and de-transition twice before she was 21. 'The second time, I made an attempt and nearly killed myself because it was either that or complete rejection,' she said.

She had panic attacks, became a recluse and began drinking and taking drugs until, at 22, she started going out to clubs in London, where she met other trans women and at last found the support she needed to feel OK about herself. But when she had gender affirming surgery in her twenties, there was no one from her family to wish her luck or hold her hand. 'No one cared but I don't play the victim. I'm not a victim. I'm a survivor. Transitioning was the biggest act of self-love I could ever have given myself,' she said defiantly.

In the years since then, Jessica has had to contend with prejudice and discrimination from many sides, including anti-trans domestic abuse in more than one of her relationships.

'One guy said he had the right to hit me because I was born a man, not a woman. Those were his words and it really annoyed me because no one is born a man. I wasn't born a man and I've never been a man. But he used it as an excuse to hit me; he said it was OK because he wasn't hitting a woman.

And he wiped me of all self-worth by saying that no other man would want me or accept me because I was trans. I was already vulnerable and damaged when I met him and by the time the relationship ended I was a shell of a person.'

I'm in awe of Jessica, especially of her strength and resilience after all she's been through. She has tried talking therapy but manages her mental health issues in different ways these days – she finds it therapeutic to write music and lyrics and says, 'When I'm performing, that is my therapy.'

One of her main goals in life is to educate people and make them more aware of how to speak to others, especially if they are transgender. 'I'm a beautiful, confident women but it sucks that it's taken me a very long time to get here because I've been held back so much due to people's lack of understanding,' she said. 'Either you make something of yourself and use all the hurt that you've been through to educate people, or you choose a darker path,' she added. 'So that's why I think it is so important for a woman like myself to be that voice to educate people that trans women are women.'

Jessica's ultimate message is a broader one of empowerment and education for all, not just the trans community, and it echoes what everyone I spoke to for this chapter said in one way or another.

'At the end of the day, we're all human and we should just treat each other as human beings. Whatever gender or sexuality we are, whoever we want to love and whatever choices we make, why can't we just value people for who we are?'

There's a lot to think about and understand when it comes to sexual orientation and gender identity. But there's something simple we can all hang on to: if we stand with the LGBTQ+ community, as diverse as it is, with all its people of intersecting identities and experiences of life, we will be helping people to be happier.

And who wouldn't want that?

7

Obsessive-Compulsive Disorder

Ali, Mia and Chloe

When someone tells you that they're 'a little bit OCD', it's often another way of saying that they're super tidy or hygienic, or they've got a thing about locking their house. Or running back to see if they've left the hair straighteners on. What they're probably not saying is that they really have obsessive-compulsive disorder (OCD), an anxiety-related condition that can seriously impede their ability to function.

'It is my life. It rules my life. It ruins my life,' said Ali, who was being treated for OCD at the hospital where we were filming the BBC documentary *Back on the Psych Ward*. Ali was a patient on Seacole, the only dedicated residential ward in the NHS offering 24-hour nursing care to patients with severe OCD. The first time we met, she had been on the ward for a few weeks and was having a really tough time of it.

'I don't want to be me. I want to be somebody else living a normal typical 21-year-old's life,' she said bleakly. 'I think things have to change or I will end up killing myself.'

Like all the people I met on Seacole, Ali was a brilliant person; she was absolutely lovely. I so felt for her and wanted to find out more about the disorder that had taken over her life. Through my conversations with staff and patients on the ward, I began learning about its two main aspects: obsession and compulsion.

People struggling with OCD have unwelcome, intrusive thoughts that can be really frightening or distressing. These thoughts are persistent and repetitive and are known as obsessions. The obsessions can relate to absolutely anything, from fear of dirt, germs or death to causing harm to oneself or others. Even though they are often based on irrational fears, people with OCD feel driven to carry out ritual behaviours, known as compulsions, as a way of trying to prevent their thoughts from becoming reality.

For example, when Ali was younger, she was obsessed with thinking that her parents were going to die in a car crash. Sitting in the back seat of the family car as they approached a busy junction, she'd do a series of rituals that she believed would prevent the car from crashing, including tapping the ceiling, blinking and other body movements.

'You can tell that it's not logical but you have to do it over and over again until you feel that you've done it enough, or that you feel you're safe,' she explained. 'It's mental torture.'

One OCD sufferer I spoke to compared it to nodding at magpies. It's like a superstitious feeling taken to extremes. But if you have OCD, doing the rituals only brings temporary relief – and when the thoughts recur and become overwhelming again, so does the need to repeat them.

I think I can imagine how it feels to some extent – I have a memory of walking over a bridge in Spain when I was about eight or nine and I had a ring or earrings on – I can't remember which – and I thought, If I don't throw this ring or earrings into the water, my mum's going to die. I obviously didn't want to throw my jewellery away but I felt I had to. I also remember as a kid thinking that if I stepped on the lines on the pavement when I was walking to school, something terrible would happen. I wonder how common these thoughts are for children.

Today, I'm someone who would rather walk up 30 flights of stairs than get in a lift, even though I know it's ridiculous, and I get really, really anxious when flying. So when I visited Seacole ward with my film crew, I thought I knew something about having unfounded fears and compulsions. But I quickly realised that I had totally underestimated how complex OCD is.

Ali was living a nightmare. Her thoughts were focused around an obsession that her body was contaminated with threadworms. She was spending most of her time thinking about how to get rid of the worms, or avoid getting worms, and explained that this type of obsessive thinking in people with OCD is known as 'ruminating'.

Ali's obsession was so severe that she was taking laxatives every night and spending hours doing rituals on the toilet because she couldn't stand the idea that the worms could feed off the food inside her. The harm she was inflicting on herself had damaged her internal organs and was causing her real pain.

'I do my rituals and I bleed so much, and it scares me what I'm doing to myself, but I can't stop,' she told me. 'Even though I hate what I'm doing with a passion, I cannot stop because it gives me that relief.'

OCD is treated with cognitive behavioural therapy (CBT), which helps people explore the links between how they think, feel, behave and react to what's going on around them. Alongside CBT, they may also be offered exposure and response prevention (ERP), which helps them face the things that make them anxious without resorting to rituals. (My understanding is that's the goal, ideally. But it still feels incredibly hard to ignore those urges.) Some people with OCD may also benefit from taking medication like SSRIs (selective serotonin reuptake inhibitors). SSRIs are a type of antidepressant that increase levels of the feel-good neurotransmitter serotonin in the brain. They can't cure OCD but they can help people respond better to CBT.

On Seacole, I joined Ali for a session of exposure therapy. She was attempting to use a communal toilet and it was really tough for her, as she hadn't used a public toilet for a long time. Ali was very fearful of germs and had multi-packs of bleach and anti-bacterial spray stored up in her room so that she could carry out her cleaning compulsions. She thought she'd probably spent a couple of hundred quid on cleaning products in the past month.

Inside the communal toilet, Ali felt petrified, especially about touching any of the surfaces. Of course, you could think, 'Why is she worrying? She's only going to the toilet.' But you can't overestimate how difficult it is to apply yourself when everything within you is screaming, 'This is risky. Don't do it!'

The therapist working with Ali was aware how difficult the session would be for her.

'It's frightening for patients to hear that the way to get better is to put yourself in a horrible situation and stay with the anxiety,' she said, 'but as part of exposure response prevention [ERP], it's really about taking a huge leap of faith. So, in the toilet, it would be about not cleaning the door handles and not washing hands excessively every time she does simple actions like this, which seems simple if you're not suffering from OCD, but obviously for her, it's very anxiety-provoking to just stay with that uncertainty and take the risk.'

As scared as she was, Ali understood how this kind of therapy might help her overcome her fears.

'Your anxiety will be very, very high and then it will get gradually less,' she explained. 'And then the next time you do it, it will be a bit less, until it feels like there is no anxiety after doing it at all.'

Several weeks later, Ali seemed brighter and more confident than when I'd last spent time with her. Her treatment seemed to be working for her. She recalled a breakthrough moment that came after her therapist did an internet search for threadworms: 'I saw a picture on her computer and I just burst into tears,' she said. 'And that made me think, "Oh my God, I need to change this, because I've been here, like, five months now and I'm still that scared, and that's not normal."'

She began by writing 'I have worms' on a piece of paper and putting it up on the wall of her room. Then she searched for pictures of worms, printed the images and put them up too, along with a photo of the inside of someone's colon.

'So you're giving yourself exposure therapy!' I said.

Next, Ali showed me something that really blew me away: a glass box containing garden worms that she and her therapist had dug out of the soil in the hospital grounds. It was amazing to see, as there's no way she would have kept anything like that in her room a couple of months earlier, when her fear of worms had taken over her life.

She said it hadn't been easy. 'The first night I had them in here, I thought, "They're going to be all over my walls, on my floor. They're going to be in my bed when I wake up in the morning."'

It was her worst fear – like a scene from a horror movie – but when she woke up, the worms were still in their box. She began learning to live with them.

I thought Ali was remarkable and brave. She'd put so much work into her recovery that she'd gone from existing, rather than living, to having pictures of the things that petrified her all over her walls and worms in her bedroom while she slept. She had every reason to be proud of herself and I felt really hopeful that she would continue to get better.

She felt more cautious about her recovery, though. 'I think, "When's it going to get bad again? When am I going to be so stressed out that the thing I resort to is what I used to do?"' she said.

What I realised during my time working on the *Psych Ward* documentaries is that there's rarely a neat beginning, middle and end to mental health problems. And, as with many other conditions, recovery from OCD is not necessarily linear or absolute.

'Recovery will mean different things to different people,' said Ashley, who works for OCD-UK, one of the leading charities providing help and support to people struggling with the disorder. 'I'm one of the people who believes that complete recovery from OCD is possible in the right set of circumstances. For other people, they can completely regain their quality of life and the OCD might still be there but they can still recover to some extent. That might be in stages: 10 per cent better, 20 per cent better, and so on.'

OCD-UK is run by people who have had the disorder and know what it feels like. Ashley could recall having symptoms from about the age of 12. 'But they were not what I would call show-stopping,' he said. 'It was only when I started work around the age of 18 that the OCD started to significantly impact on my quality of functioning – and it just got gradually worse.'

Back then, the internet didn't exist and OCD was never talked about, so it wasn't until his mid-twenties that Ashley was able to put a name to it – when a character on an episode of *Casualty* showed symptoms he recognised and was diagnosed with OCD.

'But, being a typical bloke, I didn't do anything about it,' Ashley said. 'People of my generation grew up not talking about feelings, so it took me another decade before I did actually reach out for help.'

Although OCD is only slightly more prevalent in women than men, he said that the majority of people that approach OCD-UK for help are women. 'We know as a charity that we've got to do more to reach out to men, especially young men, to talk about it,' he told me. 'I realise, looking back

20 years, that what held me back from getting help was the false belief that men don't talk about feelings; I should have reached out for help 10 years before I did.'

As part of the treatment he was eventually able to access, Ashley had exposure therapy around his obsession, which focused on germs and going to the toilet. 'I can do a lot of things now that I wasn't able to do for the better part of two decades: I can put my hand in toilet water; I can lick the sole of my shoe,' he said. 'But there's one specific issue around my OCD that I haven't yet dealt with. So I describe myself as about 80 per cent better but I'm determined to get to that 100 per cent mark.'

I wondered whether he thought that exposure therapy was the most effective way of treating OCD.

'CBT and exposure therapy are both needed, rather than just one or the other,' he cautioned. 'Often OCD is driven by the doubt and the guilt that the thoughts make us have about ourselves, so if we only treated rituals and behaviours, a person probably wouldn't recover. It's equally important to look at the cognitive side of it as part of the CBT, exploring the interpretation that we give our thoughts, the underlying beliefs around them and the emotions that we attach to them.'

One reason why OCD is so complex – and sometimes difficult to diagnose and to treat – is because it can affect people in many different ways. Even when people's ritual behaviours look the same, the reasons behind them may be poles apart.

For instance, Ali's room was full of cleaning products because she was petrified of getting threadworms; someone else's obsessions around germs might stem from a fear of passing an illness to their loved ones, or of food poisoning.

'Deep down, it's less about the fear of germs than the consequences of the germs,' Ashley said. 'It's not so much about the intrusive thoughts that we have, it's about the interpretation that we give intrusive thoughts.'

Ashley put me in touch with Mia, another of the three-quarters of a million people in the UK who are affected by OCD. Mia, who is now 18, began having OCD around the age of 8. I asked her if she would be happy to talk me through her experience, right from the beginning.

Mia vividly remembers how her OCD started. She was in Year 4 at school and it was the last day of term before the summer holidays. While using a computer in the ICT department, she became convinced that she had accidentally bought and downloaded some music on the school account, at huge expense. Unfortunately, she didn't have an opportunity to check if it was true and went home feeling worried that she had done something terrible.

'In my head, I associated the whole situation with squares because a computer is like a square,' she said, 'and so for the whole summer holidays I felt this great, overwhelming anxiety every time I went near anything square. I didn't tell anyone, because I thought I was going to be in so much trouble; I turned it into a compulsion, which was avoiding squares.'

She had no idea that she had OCD. 'I remember lying down when my parents weren't around and just crying and looking up at the ceiling because I did not understand what was happening to me,' she said. 'I started doing this routine before I went to bed, where I would go through everything bad I thought I'd done in my life and say it over and over again. If I didn't do it, I didn't know what would happen. That's when those habits started and gradually they've increased.'

In Year 5 and Year 6 at school, Mia developed a fear of a particular teacher and associated their lesson with having a distressing thought.

'A normal person without OCD will have a thought and it will be: "Oh, that's not very nice." Then they move on with their day or their life,' she explained. 'But it's as if someone with OCD has a spider web in their head; the thought gets attached and it takes a very long time for the thought to leave, if it ever does. That's the difference – it sticks around. And that's when it becomes so horrible and turns into obsessions and compulsions, anxiety and panic attacks.'

Around this time, Mia began to realise that her peers weren't affected by the worries she was having, especially in the run up to a school trip to Wales at the end of Year 6.

'Everyone was excited about it but I did not want to go. It was weird seeing everyone else wanting to do something that

I was really worried about doing. In the end I went but I hated the whole trip; I had so much anxiety.

'On the last day of the trip, I remember feeling not real. This is what I know now to be "derealisation", which is when you're so overwhelmed with anxiety that you detach yourself and don't feel like you're in reality. It's a really horrible feeling. Everything around me felt distant and I just didn't feel normal.'

Back in her bedroom at home, Mia convinced herself that she was going to wake up in Wales the next morning. 'It was something that could never happen but in my head it was going to. My brain was being pushed to the extreme and I thought, "I'm still there. This is not real." And it felt like that for a very, very long time – for months.'

Thoughts like these are known as 'magical thinking', she explained. 'There's no part of OCD that is realistic but this was completely unrealistic and I didn't really know how to talk about it because it sounded so crazy. At that age, you can't really put things into perspective or see things clearly. I went on to have a lot of magical thinking about really bizarre things that brought me so much distress: that I was going to wake up really tiny and everybody would forget about me; that I would wake up and my mum wouldn't know who I was or I would wake up with dead bodies taped to my wall.'

Around the age of 12, just before she was diagnosed with OCD, Mia read in the news about a woman who had no idea she was pregnant and gave birth while sitting on the toilet.

Convinced that the same thing could happen to her, even though it wasn't possible, for the next year Mia checked for signs of a baby every time she went to the toilet.

In secondary school, she had obsessive thinking around wetting herself in front of everyone; she always sat on her jacket, just in case it happened. Another strong compulsion was the need to inspect every surface of a room she went into because she was worried she had written something inappropriate on the wall and someone would find it. As this obsession became heavier, she started to check every side and surface of every object she came into contact with, and then began checking all round her bedroom for signs of scratches.

'My bedtime routine could take up to an hour of checking every single surface. If I didn't do it right, I'd have to completely do it all over again and that was so exhausting.'

She found it increasingly difficult to leave the house. 'Secondary school became too much,' she recalled. 'When it came to my schoolwork, I was doing so many different compulsions that it was distressing and I couldn't focus.'

Finally, she decided that she had to tell someone about it. 'One night I broke down to my mum in my room. My mum didn't know what it was but then my dad came upstairs and he knew straight away because he has OCD. He never told anyone or got help for it – when he was growing up in the eighties it wasn't spoken about – but he has very similar obsessions and behaviours. I'm actually very thankful that I have someone who knows about it; he understands the thoughts I'm getting and why I'm doing the compulsions.'

Mia went on the waiting list for the Child and Adolescent Mental Health Services (CAMHS) in her area and started doing half days at school. After half a term, she stopped going to school altogether.

'It was so overwhelming that I couldn't do it anymore. I never talked about it – I was too embarrassed – and I was trying to hide my compulsions because they looked a bit weird. Naturally, people asked questions and I didn't have the answers. That was about five years ago now and it has been a nightmare ever since.'

Ashley at OCD-UK is concerned that too few youth mental health workers recognise the severity of OCD.

'The number of parents who have contacted OCD-UK and said to me, "CAMHS have said they won't escalate treatment because my young person is not self-harming or suicidal,"' he said. 'And 18 months later, that young person still hasn't had treatment. Some people just don't realise that the compulsions we do are self-harming from day one, not just 18 months later – and if treatment isn't given quickly enough, a person could become significantly worse.'

He pointed out that OCD can be severe to the point where it literally stops a person functioning: 'Basic everyday bodily functions, like going to a toilet, can become a nightmarish journey for some young people and prevent them living their life how they want. They might somehow get themselves to school. But that's a massive challenge. And then there's no life beyond that.'

As much as anything, OCD is an anxiety disorder. In 2017, when Mia was 14, she went on a family holiday. 'I told myself I could do it but the morning I got up to go to the airport with my family, I had probably the worst panic attack of my life. I was completely paralysed: I couldn't walk; I couldn't speak.'

I wondered if she could describe to me how her panic feels.

'A lot of people describe panic attacks as feeling like you're dying and I've thought that I needed an ambulance multiple times,' she said. 'It's like my legs have turned to jelly. I can't feel my hands. I get a tingling sensation in my face, around my lips. I go white. My eyes go really blurry. I see spots and can't focus properly. My heart races and I feel really dizzy. It's the worst feeling – I really can't explain how horrible it is but I want people to know that they're not alone, that anxiety is quite common and that help is out there.'

With her parents' help and a wheelchair service at the airport, Mia managed to get on the plane and to their holiday villa but she stayed inside the villa all week. Then, after another serious panic attack on the way home, she began to experience PTSD flashbacks that were triggered by anything to do with airports and travel.

'It was bizarre,' she said, 'because you think PTSD is experienced by people who go away to fight in the army and see really traumatic things. You don't expect to have it after going on holiday, which is supposed to be a nice thing.'

To calm herself down, Mia uses a technique called 54321, where you focus on five things you can see, four things you can feel, three things you can hear, two things you can smell and one thing you can taste.

'It's about trying to ground yourself because anxiety feels like you're floating away, if that makes sense; being able to feel like you're present is a massive part of beating anxiety. But sometimes it can get to the point where nothing helps and you just have to ride the wave. I've learnt over the years that sometimes the more you fight the anxiety, the worse it gets, so in that case I lie down, close my eyes and just let it be.'

I asked her what her compulsions look like now. She explained that they were focused around the numbers one to ten, with a thought for every number. Each thought is completely different to the other and there are good numbers and bad numbers depending on the day. On the day we spoke, her bad numbers were 4, 5, 8, 9 and 10, and she had issues with fingers and toes that corresponded to these numbers. On alternate days, the bad numbers would be good numbers.

'Today is what I'd say is a heavier day,' she told me, holding up one hand, 'so I can't touch anything with this thumb or my fifth toe all day. If I touched something with this thumb, it would bring so much anxiety that I'd have to do some sort of bargaining deal with my OCD and do something else to make it OK. And when I'm walking, I see a timeline in my head and I will walk on the numbers that are OK.'

It must be absolutely exhausting for her, I said. I wondered how much of the time it was happening, or was it all the time? I knew from the people I'd met on Seacole that often there's no respite.

'All the time,' she said. 'Usually there's a main thought that's really bugging me and little triggers throughout the day can make that thought much louder.'

I really felt for her. Life's hard enough – you're just trying to navigate your way through, aren't you? And then you've got this crippling disorder to try to contend with on top of the more familiar day-to-day issues.

'It makes everything very, very hard,' she agreed. 'A thought will come into my head randomly that says, "You have to hold your breath until you enter that room." If I'm upstairs, I have to hold my breath all the way downstairs and that's not healthy for anyone.'

I asked her what happens if she doesn't carry out a compulsion. She said it felt like being stuck in mud or glue.

'It's almost like a magnet: I can't move until I do it,' she said. 'And it's the most uncomfortable feeling if I don't do it – it doesn't feel right. Reassurance is the worst thing someone else can do because I already know that doing the compulsions is not going to change anything. It makes it hard to explain because people think, "Why do it if you know nothing is going to happen if you don't?" But it's just such a weird feeling if you don't do it.'

It reminded me of something Ashley at OCD-UK had said: 'It's about control and trying to prevent the perceived risk that we've interpreted.'

Mia offered to talk me through some of the thoughts she felt comfortable sharing.

'They can be quite dark but they are thoughts and please don't think any differently of me,' she said. 'I'm just going to be honest.'

It was brave of her to share them with me and I really appreciated her candour.

'I want to spread awareness,' she said. 'There are so many subtypes and themes in OCD that people just wouldn't think of as OCD. The stereotypical one is contamination and cleaning but that is just 1 per cent of what OCD is.' She wasn't comfy talking about all of her thoughts, so she began by describing what she calls her thought number two, which is all around self-harm or anything to do with violence, knives, and hurting people. 'It sounds really weird, I know,' she said.

Thought number three is a subtype of OCD that focuses on feeling responsible for other people.

'This really torments me: I have the biggest fear of upsetting or hurting people. I've got my main friends that I feel comfortable with and that I've known forever, but when I start making new friends, I panic and think, I don't want to hurt this person. I feel like if I don't talk to them every day, or every other day, I'm a bad person, and I can't deal with it.'

Mia's number three thought reminded me of something a psychiatrist I met at Seacole had said. She had noted that it was a common personality trait in her OCD patients to be remarkably conscientious. Although everyone is different, she said, people with OCD tend to prioritise other people and are very empathic.

'I hate thinking I've said something wrong or offended anyone,' Mia said.

Her number five thought is around body dysmorphia, which she says is a slightly different OCD subtype because it is its own disorder (people can have body dysmorphia without having OCD). This thought started in 2020.

'It's the main thought that is terrorising me at the moment,' she said. 'It's the one that makes me the saddest and it's the hardest to combat because someone can say, "Oh, you're pretty; you don't need to worry," and it doesn't do a thing. There's nothing that can stop these thoughts. They're always there. They don't go away.'

Her number six thought is everything to do with her mum, including her mum being disappointed in her, or being ill. Number eight is anything to do with her dad. 'Same thing goes. It's just as devastating and hard,' she said.

Number ten is an example of 'real event OCD', she explained. 'These are things that have happened that you will ruminate over and just never really get over. There's an incident that happened last year and I don't really want to talk about it. Number ten is to do with that and is really, really hard.'

Mia has been taking sertraline, an SSRI, since she was 14 but has found it harder to access CBT since she moved from CAMHS to adult mental health services when she turned 18. She's had an application for funding rejected and was hoping to appeal – I hope she gets there because she has so much she wants to do in life and it's heartbreaking to see how OCD is holding her back.

'Just being able to go out of the house and do normal things has been hard, even though I've really, really wanted to,' she said. 'It's debilitating and yet I'm still trying to do the things I want to do, despite having OCD.'

I was so grateful to Mia for sharing her story because I know it will help other people. She is an ambassador for OCD-UK and has already done loads of great work on the charity's website, including interviewing other people with OCD. She also has her own mental health page on Instagram and I'm in awe of how brave she is to share her experiences on social media. The power of her transparency can't be overestimated – just posting on her Instagram page will have changed people's lives. Her open approach made me mindful of something Ali had said when she agreed to be part of our film: 'I just want to help and if sharing my story will even help one person the tiniest bit, that for me is huge and makes it worth it.'

While we were making *Back on the Psych Ward*, I was hoping to meet someone who had come out the other side of OCD and recovered. So it was good to be introduced to Chloe, who had been discharged from Seacole just before lockdown began in 2020.

Chloe was 15 when her OCD got so bad that it had made her suicidal. Her most intrusive thought was around harm coming to her family: she would be scared to touch things or leave the house; she was constantly fearful that someone had passed by and given her something that she could pass on.

'The obsessions and the rituals started to take over my life and I couldn't think about anything else,' she recalled. 'And there was a point where I decided that the only way out of it was to end my life.'

I asked her how the therapy at Seacole helped. She felt that exposure therapy had worked for her and told me about a concept called the pendulum effect. She asked me to imagine a swinging pendulum: on one side is 'living with OCD'; in the middle is 'normal behaviour'; and on the other side you have 'the extreme opposite of OCD'. The idea during therapy is to swing the pendulum from 'living with OCD' to its extreme opposite, in order for it to sit back in the middle.

'So I would be encouraged to do horrific things like put my hand down the toilet and all in my hair and round my mouth,' she said. 'I've spoken to a lot of people since that don't suffer with OCD and they've been like, "I couldn't do that!"' (Which was my exact reaction!)

By talking on film, Chloe wanted to highlight that there is hope in every situation. 'I was at the lowest of the low. I never thought I would ever live a life without OCD and I am, I'm living it,' she said. 'I never thought I'd be able to live at home again, never thought I was getting out of hospital.'

If Chloe was in any doubt about the strength of her recovery, she had a pandemic to test her resilience when she finally came out, after four years spent in various hospitals.

'I was just building my life up again. Then it's like, "You've got to stay at home now, got to quarantine; lockdown is happening; you can't go out."'

Suddenly, she found herself exposed to TV adverts that played on her fears. Slogans like, 'Keep your family safe by washing your hands,' spoke directly to her OCD.

'It just completely blew my mind,' she said.

But her recovery was strong and she got through it. She is now at university.

Chloe told me that she felt indebted to the staff at Seacole for the therapy and tools they gave her while she was there. Certainly, I found their dedication and expertise really impressive and couldn't help thinking that perhaps there should be more than one residential ward for people with severe OCD in the whole of the UK – bearing in mind that the waiting list for places on Seacole has shot up dramatically since lockdown.

Chloe summed up how vital a place like Seacole can be.

'I've had to work hard but without this place, I dread to think where I'd be,' she said. 'I don't know if I'd be alive.'

8

Gambling Addiction

Matt

Ask most people what springs to mind when they think of addiction and the chances are that they'll say tobacco, drugs or alcohol. Thanks to health campaigns and addiction storylines in films and on screen, we know quite a bit about the dangers of substance abuse. What we don't seem as aware of is that a flutter at the bookies can be every bit as high risk as taking certain drugs, even though the latest edition of the *Diagnostic and Statistical Manual of Mental Disorders* (*DSM-5*), the mental health bible, places gambling disorder in its own category among addictions.

Matt, an ex-gambler, wishes that he'd understood the risks when he started gambling 11 years ago at the age of 16. (I was shocked at how young he started. I stupidly and ignorantly associated gambling with adults.) But back then, he was just having fun, he told me: he bought scratch cards and sneaked the occasional bet at the bookies, despite being under the legal age.

Matt got further into betting when he went to university to do a performing arts degree and played for his uni football team. Still, it was fun, he said.

'Sunday morning: 15 lads would play football; we'd go home and shower, meet at the pub, watch the Premier League games and place bets at the bookies a few doors down.'

Soon he discovered fixed odds betting terminals, the touch screen machines you often find inside bookmakers; he started playing virtual roulette and then virtual blackjack. It was a boost to his finances when he won. 'At the time, as a student, if you won 50 or 60 quid it would see you through the next week,' he recalled. 'But I didn't identify that I was probably losing a bit more than I was winning.'

Fixed odds betting terminals have been linked to high rates of addiction and critics talk about them as the 'crack cocaine' of gambling. But Matt reckoned that his betting wasn't problematic at this point. 'I was gambling more than the average student, but it was something I enjoyed.'

Gambling became more of a serious issue midway through his third year at university, when he started to play live casino blackjack on his laptop. Online gambling sucked him in quickly; he began to think that it was something he shouldn't be doing and that maybe he should speak to someone about it. Only, when he looked around him, his mates were all doing it too, so he kept quiet. 'I didn't want to be the guy that went there with a problem, so I carried on.'

Matt left uni at 21, got an acting agent and went away on tour. 'That was the turning point, when a small problem started affecting many areas of my life,' he said. 'I wasn't in that culture of people anymore, yet I was still gambling, even though I didn't need the winnings because I was earning good money.'

Over the next two years, when he wasn't away touring, he lived at home with his parents between jobs and went on gambling.

'I didn't think it was escapism at the time, but when I wasn't working, I was bored and aimless. Gambling gave me a sense of purpose and took away the feeling of being a jobless performer.'

Things escalated from there. At his worst, he was on his laptop for 16 or 17 hours a day, depositing up to £5,000 a day on betting sites. His parents didn't suspect a thing.

'I was very sneaky about how I did it,' he told me. 'I had a bit of a routine: they would get up at five in the morning, so I would gamble all night. At five in the morning, I'd shut my laptop, slide it under the bed and pretend to be asleep. Then, the minute they left for work, I'd gamble all day until they got home. In the evening, I'd have a few hours with them, eating dinner, watching telly and doing the normal things you do with your family, and the minute they went to bed I'd go back on it again.'

It's amazing that no one twigged, but then I suppose it's quite easy to hide online gambling. 'That's where problems can really escalate,' according to Matt.

If he'd been drinking or taking drugs in his room, his folks would probably have noticed. But if you're sober and you're coming down for dinner in the evening, no one's going to see a problem. It's why gambling is often called 'the hidden addiction'.

I had to admit to Matt that I've merely flirted with gambling (did, like, $80 in Vegas and a syndicate on the footie once) and asked him if he could describe the sensation it gives you. I'd read that gambling triggers the brain's reward system and releases the feel-good hormone dopamine into the body, sometimes up to ten times the normal amount, which must feel amazing. 'When you win money and you're up, at that moment do you feel totally elated?' I asked.

I assumed that it's the euphoria that keeps you coming back for more but Matt said that it's as much about the anticipation as it is about winning money. The suspense and the risk are what's really exciting and trigger the dopamine: when you're thinking, 'Am I going to win or not going to win? Am I going to lose everything?'

'Of course, winning £1,000 in 30 seconds does feel great,' he told me. 'You think, I've just earned half a month's wages in 30 seconds! If I keep doing this, I'm going to be a millionaire. But when you lose, you still want to go back because there is a chemical reaction neurologically that makes you enjoy that feeling of anticipation.'

Hearing this brought back the days when my mum and I lived in Luton, and she used to run a pub. There was a fruit machine in the pub and, because she was working behind the bar, she knew exactly what was going into the machine. So, after Bob put this amount in and Dave put this amount in, she thought she had an idea of when it was going to pay out.

When I went to visit her at work, she'd be on the machine. 'How much have you put in there, Mum?' I'd ask.

'It's due to pay out any moment!' she'd say.

She thought she was being methodical about it and knew what she was doing: she wasn't being played; she was the one playing. But of course she never really won.

'That's why it can happen to anyone,' Matt says. 'There were points in my journey when I thought, "I've worked this out."'

He didn't see himself as an addict. 'Unfortunately, there's still a stigma around addiction in this country. When you think about an addict, you think about someone who might not be very well educated; they might not dress very well, and all these things.

'I thought, "I'm smarter than that."'

But as gambling took over his life, his self-esteem plummeted.

'I guess the thing I didn't identify was that there was a lot of depression building up over those two years. The gambling was making me feel pretty bad about myself. I'd lost all control by this point and the feeling of being out of control of something that everyone else could control was really, really difficult.'

He blamed himself. 'I thought, "This is just me. I'm the only person who is taking it too far. Why can't I control gambling like everyone else can?" What I didn't know at the time was that there were hundreds of thousands of people in a very similar situation to me.'

Studies show that brain chemistry and cell structure can be seriously affected by prolonged exposure to online gambling. The first thing on the list of indicators for gambling disorder given by the latest edition of the *Diagnostic and Statistical Manual of Mental Disorders* is the need 'to gamble with increasing amounts of money in order to achieve the desired excitement'.

By the time Matt was gambling 17 hours a day, he had developed a tolerance for the surges of dopamine that had originally hooked him in. Gambling wasn't giving him the same thrill it once had; his brain's reward centre had become weaker and he needed to gamble for longer periods and take bigger risks to trigger the dopamine levels he was used to and now craved. His decision-making was governed by risk and he was constantly chasing losses. It reached a point where there wasn't room for anything else in Matt's life apart from online betting.

Things came to a head in February 2016, when he was 22. 'I was gambling my normal amount and I put my savings in, not expecting to lose it, and I lost it all very, very quickly.

I then panicked and took out the biggest overdraft I could from my bank account and placed all of that, and lost all of that,' he recalls.

Just like that, he had no money left.

'It was a horrible feeling. I remember quite vividly lying in bed and thinking, "This is a problem that I'm not in control of. This is me now. This is my life for the next 40 or 50 years." Since no one else knew about it, my lack of control was only really causing me harm. But I couldn't stop thinking about how one day I'd grow up and have a wife and maybe some children, and how my lack of control would affect these two or three other people. The shame and guilt of potentially making three other people feel like that – that was for me what pushed me over the edge. There was also the shame of what my parents would think; no one wants their parents to be disappointed in them or to think they can't cope with life. But mainly I was thinking of the future. I felt there was no way out, that the only way I would stop this addiction was if I stopped myself.

'In total despair, the next morning, I drove to my local town centre and jumped off a six-storey car park in a quite serious attempt on my life. I broke every bone in my left foot, crushed my pelvis, broke all my ribs, broke my wrist, damaged nerves in my head and vertebrae in my back. Every bone you could mention, I've probably broken or damaged it. Obviously, I'm lucky I survived, and I'm lucky I'm quite mobile and can still walk.'

Luck was on his side – in the best possible way. Others haven't been so fortunate and it's estimated that several hundred suicides every year are gambling related. As yet there isn't enough data to put an actual figure on it because of the way coroners record deaths.

So when and why does gambling cross over from a bit of fun to becoming an addiction – and is the problem getting worse?

Back in the 1960s, betting had a reputation for being a bit shady. Bookmakers' windows were blacked out. Having a problem with gambling was seen as a moral failing and a large section of society disapproved of any kind of betting. Attitudes slowly relaxed over the decades and then Labour liberalised gambling in Britain with the 2005 Gambling Act, which led to a massive increase in betting activities across the country. At the time, there was a lot of concern about giant gambling hubs known as super casinos springing up. What actually happened was that people started gambling online and on smartphones in huge numbers.

The lowest estimate I've found for problem gamblers in the UK is 280,000, according to a study by NHS Digital. Other estimates vary wildly: it could be 400,000, 580,000 or many more, depending whose numbers you look at. A 2018 YouGov survey commissioned by the GambleAware charity suggested that the figure could be as high as 1.4 million, or 2.7 per cent of the population. Whether you take the lowest or highest estimate, it's a lot of people potentially experiencing debt, destitution, relationship break-ups, anxiety, sleeplessness, depression, low self-esteem, self-loathing and despair – even suicide.

The 24-hour National Gambling Helpline (0808 8020 133) logged nearly 42,000 callers in 2020, the last time they were able to collate figures. Of the gamblers who contacted them, a quarter talked about the impact that betting had on their mental health; 11 per cent admitted to having suicidal thoughts, either at the time or over the previous two years.

For every person with a gambling problem, between six and ten other people are likely to be impacted, sometimes as seriously as the gambler. Among the helpline callers who were affected by someone else's gambling, including family members, partners and friends, more than half were experiencing significant stress and anxiety. The strain on marriages and family relationships is often unbearable.

Men are seven times more likely to become problem gamblers, maybe because they are hardwired to take risks or because they are more exposed to gambling culture and promotion by watching more sport. The profile of callers to the National Gambling Helpline tends to contradict the image Matt had of your typical addict, though. Callers come from all kinds of backgrounds and are more likely than not to be employed, in a relationship or married; like Matt, many online gamblers who call the helpline are from higher education backgrounds and work in professional or managerial roles.

'I would never have believed it could happen to anyone until it happened to me,' he said. 'When I was 16, everything told me that if I chose a pathway of taking heroin, it wouldn't work out well. With gambling, we don't have that kind of awareness.'

Unlike heroin, gambling is legal – and there is a side to it that is seen as exciting and joyful. 'Ah, have a flutter! Let's have fun, bet on a match, get a scratch card …' The ads you see on the telly and on billboards show people celebrating. You never see anyone with their head in their hands, in despair that they've lost all their savings. Yet gamblers in the UK lose £10.2 billion a year.

Over £10 billion a year. Staggering.

Winning is always a possibility but when you get to the level of intense gambling that Matt reached, the chances are that you're headed for a fall, according to Catherine, who was the head of communications at the gambling charity GamCare when we spoke in late 2020. GamCare runs the National Gambling Helpline and is funded by voluntary contributions by the gambling industry.

'One of our key messages is that the longer you gamble, the more you are likely to lose,' Catherine said. 'It's not a way to make money. It's not about being smart. You can't affect chance.'

As Matt pointed out, 'If you keep taking heroin or cocaine, it's never going to come to a good outcome but with gambling there's always that chance. People go on that small belief that they might hit the jackpot and they take it further and further.'

Do the gambling ads ever address this, though? Critics say that by advising people to gamble responsibly, they put the burden on the individual – by implication, anyone who becomes addicted is basically just being irresponsible. So people blame themselves when their gambling spirals out of control – as Matt did. You're told to 'stop when the fun stops' and yet it's at that moment that you will likely have developed a gambling disorder, so you probably won't be able to stop without help and treatment.

Gambling advertising is everywhere: you see it in some form or another on telly, online, at the train station, when you're watching football and on billboards by the roadside. You can't get away from it, which must be torture if you're trying to recover from a gambling disorder. It's like advertising alcohol to a recovering alcoholic or cigarettes to an ex-smoker.

'The majority of our services users would tell us that the volume of advertising around gambling, not just on television but in other areas, isn't helpful if they are trying to step away, or if they are trying to control their gambling,' Catherine told me.

A 2021 YouGov survey for the Royal Society for Public Health found that the majority of the public support a total ban on gambling ads and many are in favour of not allowing them before the watershed on TV and radio, along with the kind of online promotion that draws in younger people.

I've seen reports in the past where certain MPs and campaigners have had real issues with where betting shops are placed geographically, in more deprived areas, where disposable income is a lot lower than in other areas. A recent study showed that some of the UK's poorest areas have more than ten times the number of betting shops than the most affluent areas; Matt told me that there are two William Hills, two Corals, a Ladbrokes and a BetFred on his local high street in Kent.

'Local authorities need to do risk assessments before they can grant licences,' Catherine suggested. 'They need to take a holistic view and ask, "How close is the new outlet to schools? What time do they open?" Local communities can contribute and say, "We don't think it's good for our area."'

'For me, it's about the education around gambling,' Matt added. 'In fact, if people had the education, you'd have fewer shops because people would either not gamble or be a lot more controlled than they are.'

But the fact is that children and young people see gambling promoted on telly and billboards all the time. Campaigners in favour of tougher restrictions have likened it to being groomed. If you're then telling them that gambling can be dangerous, isn't it confusing?

One really alarming statistic is that around 55,000 young people aged 11 to 16 either could already be classed as having an issue or would be at risk – kids who are playing anything from 'penny up against the wall' in the playground to slot machines in the arcade. In-game micro-transactional gambling is on the rise among teenage gamers and has been linked to problem gambling; loot boxes, mystery 'boxes' containing random prizes that can be opened by playing the game or paid for with real money, are another growing phenomenon and can encourage virtual gambling among even very young players. In 2018, a Gambling Commission audit found that youngsters were staking an average of £16 a week on fruit machines, bingo, betting shops and online games, which are all illegal if you are under 18. More children said they had placed a bet in the past week than had drunk alcohol, smoked or taken drugs.

Matt's first role at GamCare was on their youth programme, Big Deal, helping young people understand the risks that are associated with gambling.

'We need to be more aware of these statistics as a society,' he said. 'Youth programmes are often centred around alcohol, substance misuse and sexual health – and that's all great work but young people are spending more money on gambling than tobacco, yet we're talking to them about smoking and illegal drugs. Personally I put that down to people not having the knowledge to be confident speaking about gambling.'

As well as providing support and treatment for people who are already affected by gambling addiction, GamCare has outreach and education programmes for young people in conjunction with another organisation called YGAM, Young Gamers and Gamblers Education Trust.

Asking GPs and school teachers to be aware of how their patients or pupils might be harmed by gambling or a parent's gambling is a key part of the programmes. 'We would always say that unless a young person understands what gambling is and what the risks are, and unless we can open up those wider conversations around gambling and make sure that it isn't a taboo subject – and actually it is OK to ask questions around what is safe and what is not – it is a significant concern for us, which is where our outreach and education programmes come in and, more recently, our dedicated treatment services for young people. So as of this year we are specifically offering treatment services for under-16s as well,' Catherine said.

It sounds like great work but somehow it doesn't make sense. The machines, betting shops, scratch cards, high-profile promotion and ads are designed to get people gambling, absolutely legally, and yet under-16s are being treated for gambling problems. Something is going wrong.

As Dr Matt Gaskell, clinical lead and consultant psychologist for the NHS Northern Gambling Service, tweeted in the summer of 2021, 'The gambling industry, in its modern form, is a clear and present danger to the public health of our communities. Only the government can cut it down to size by ripping up our outdated laws and introducing a comprehensive set of "prevention first" policies.'

At the time of writing, a government review of the 2005 Gambling Act was expected soon, with MPs and Lords on all sides of the political spectrum pushing for new controls. That being said, there are concerns about the might and connections of the gambling lobby. At the last count, the gambling industry was worth more than £15 billion a year. Of that, the UK government takes around £3 billion in taxes.

Along with a ban on advertising, campaigners are suggesting a product classification system that grades different forms of gambling according to the known characteristics that make them addictive, like speed of play and stake sizes (on the different categories of fixed odds betting terminals), and affordability checks conducted by online gambling operators to make sure that gamblers are able to afford their losses.

I'm mindful that a lot of the people who call the National Gambling Helpline will be in debt, which must put a horrific strain on their mental state.

'If you gamble your overdraft and then realise that it's going to take you four months of work to pay it back but you're out of work, it's stressful,' Matt agreed.

'In one way, it's helpful in most cases when people come to us with debt issues,' Catherine said, 'because it's the catalyst for them getting in touch and realising that there's a problem here that they're going to have to address – and own up to their loved ones. They may have taken out an extra mortgage or spent a loan, or there's a new baby on the way and they've spent their savings cushion. It can be that those crisis points lead to people reaching out but obviously we want to reach them before the crisis comes.'

We associate success with having money and knowing how to manage money, and there's a level of respect for people who are sensible with their finances. So, if you go off the course that society expects of adults, you're going to feel ashamed or embarrassed, aren't you? I imagine there's nothing worse than lying awake at 3am thinking, 'The mortgage is coming out on the third and my partner doesn't know there's no money.'

'That's one of the reasons the helpline is available round the clock,' Catherine told me.

What happens when you reach out for help? What sort of treatment works? At the NHS Northern Gambling Service, they use group and one-to-one cognitive behavioural therapy to help gambling addicts to recover. If you ring their helpline, you'll speak to someone trained in this specific addiction who may well have lived experience of problem gambling. As yet there are only a handful of these clinics – all funded or partly funded by contributions from the gambling industry; still, the government has said that up to 14 new NHS clinics are in the pipeline. It's a promise that they need to deliver on if existing problem gambling is to be tackled.

I asked Matt how he found his way to recovery.

'I recovered in a unique way,' he says. 'I was put into a physical situation where I was in hospital for three months, with no access to internet, so I couldn't gamble. I didn't have any behavioural therapy but I'm lucky to have an amazing family and I always say to people that I did my "talking therapy" with my family. Once I had exposed all the lies I'd told and they knew what was going on, the weight lifted off me.'

When he left hospital and got his phone back, he put safeguards in place to make sure he didn't go back to gambling. You can make accessing gambling websites and apps more difficult for yourself by installing a type of software on your device through GamCare's TalkBanStop project, which Matt now manages. You can also register with GAMSTOP UK and you won't be able to access your gaming accounts for anything between six months and five years.

And there are other ways to protect yourself against relapse, Matt says. 'Before I got married in 2021, I had to have a very honest conversation with my fiancée about what had happened because she wasn't around at the time. We were starting a life together and one thing I was really keen on was our finances being shared. Part of that is because I want to start a life with her. Another part is if I ever took any money out to gamble, she would immediately see. I'm hopeful that I won't go back to gambling but I'm not stupid enough to think that it could never happen. It's about putting safeguards in place.'

Matt started working at GamCare three years after his suicide attempt and says it was only then that he began to dissect what had happened to him. 'I walked into it thinking it wouldn't be dangerous, never imagining it could get to a point where I would be attempting suicide. Now I understand why it happened, what went wrong and what could have been put in place to potentially not reach that point.'

Although men are much more likely to become problem gamblers, I don't want to lose sight of the fact that women are also vulnerable to this addiction.

'Among the women we speak to within our services, there is a huge amount of shame in having to face up to society's expectations,' Catherine told me. 'That kind of stigma – of thinking, "I should be cleverer than this; I shouldn't find myself in this situation. How am I going to talk to people about this?" It's a really big barrier to opening up earlier on, before it gets to a crisis point.'

Attitudes to gambling haven't changed as much as we might think, according to Catherine. 'Cultural perceptions around gambling do vary throughout the country but, actually, there is quite a large section of the community that would see it as a mild failing to gamble at all.

'We are working specifically with women at the moment because there is a cultural perception that gambling is a male issue – it is a male activity – and therefore it couldn't impact on women that badly. That, again, creates another layer of stigma around the fact that, actually, women do gamble. They need to be able to access support, too, and feel comfortable to do that.'

Gambling can be seen as a spectrum or continuum of harm, she explained. There's social gambling, where it's fun and a social activity. As you progress along that, if people are becoming more engaged in gambling away from others, it's usually a way to escape from something else.

'I've heard so many people describe it as a bubble,' she said. 'When they're focused on the gambling, everything else is not important. Over the pandemic, more and more people talked about domestic abuse, and either because they were experiencing domestic abuse, they were using gambling to focus on something else and escape those feelings, or it can be a consequence of domestic abuse, when a perpetrator is feeling so guilty about their gambling that they're lashing out.

'That bubble around gambling makes it feel like it's the most important thing but actually the ripple effect outside that, and what other situations aren't being addressed, might be just as important. The impact on the gambler is one thing but it also has an impact on their loved ones.'

What Catherine said makes me think we really don't talk about this enough. When you hear that alcoholism or other issues can lead to domestic violence, you think, 'Yeah, sure.' But you don't necessarily associate it with gambling.

I'm well aware of the impact a friend or family member's addiction can have on the people close to them because I have a relative who, a couple of years ago, was in a bad situation through gambling. They were trying look flash but were actually skint (as we all have been at times); they were constantly trying to keep up appearances because they had a partner who they probably felt needed a certain lifestyle to be happy. I remember them asking me, 'Can I borrow X amount?' and it puts you in a very awkward position because of course you're desperate to help and if they can give the money back then you want to lend and be generous, but are you enabling and ultimately making the situation worse?

'It's one of those difficult conversations we have to have with loved ones. If someone is struggling with gambling, we would never advise lending money. It's about having that conversation and saying, "Look, we're worried about you."' Catherine explained.

I asked her if it was right, therefore, to think that no one is exempt. Is it simply a question of being exposed to gambling or of how a person's early experiences with gambling played out? I'd heard that if you have a big win early on in your gambling journey, you're more vulnerable to becoming addicted.

'That's some of it,' she said, 'but also if at any point there are particularly strong emotions attached to gambling, good or bad, it can be an attachment that way, as well. For instance, if you're angry or upset when you start gambling, it's likely to escalate quickly.'

I asked Catherine about levels of gambling during the pandemic, when people couldn't get out to bingo or betting shops so much. Did she notice things getting better or worse?

'We would say that the key risk factors across people vulnerable to gambling harm are isolation, financial worries and boredom. All three of those things increased during the pandemic, in a variety of different combinations. Couple that with easy access to online gambling and it's a real worry.'

The social aspect of gambling is important, she added. It's one thing if you're doing it openly, with your friends, and having fun, but quite another if you're gambling in isolation, as Matt eventually was.

'I would say that's a big warning sign,' Catherine said, 'because if you're not talking to people about it – if you're hiding it from people then subconsciously you know something's not quite right.'

Clearly, having these conversations and talking about gambling is really important. There is a risk that it can become harmful and if we don't talk about it, it's only going to get worse. People need to go into it with their eyes open – and know that there is a way out if things get out of hand. The problem gamblers Matt speaks to get a lot of value out of knowing that some of this is beyond their control and the end goal is recovery. There is hope. 'A lot of people recover from gambling problems,' he told me.

Critics of the gambling industry would argue that we need to take a closer look at preventing those problems in the first place.

9

Psychosis

Sharief and Paul

When I met Sharief at Springfield hospital in autumn 2020, about six months into the Covid-19 pandemic, he was talking a lot about the devil and God.

Sharief had been sectioned and brought to the hospital after his neighbours called the police. He was being assessed in the Orchid Mental Health Emergency Service, which is essentially like an A&E for mental health. Before we sat down to talk, Jack, the clinical nurse specialist at Orchid, filled me in on Sharief's situation.

'He's got a psychotic illness. He's relapsed and is extremely unwell,' Jack said.

Psychotic disorders, including schizophrenia, affect fewer than 1 in 100 people in any given year, according to the mental health charity Mind. Unfortunately, Sharief wasn't accepting the antipsychotic medication that he'd been prescribed in the community and so had been referred for an inpatient bed.

We met in a bright, airy side room off the ward and I asked Sharief if he was happy to talk me through his understanding of psychosis. Even in crisis, he was super articulate.

'Psychosis is like a fire in the brain,' he said. 'Psychosis is a puff of madness, just a brief puff of madness and that's it.'

Bex, the unit manager at Orchid, followed up with another question. 'Sharief, do you agree with the opinion that you're relapsing in your psychosis?'

'Not at all,' he said. 'That is the opinion of Satan, that I'm relapsing, and that's how they control the knowers.'

Sharief had struggled with psychosis on and off for four years before I met him. When he arrived at Orchid, Bex and Jack recognised that he was experiencing delusional thinking: he had developed beliefs that didn't rationally make sense and was finding them really frightening. He also seemed preoccupied, as if he was constantly being distracted, and so Bex thought that he was probably experiencing auditory hallucinations or hearing voices.

'You were placed under section 2 and you know that section 2 is the section that lasts up to 28 days,' Jack said, referring to the fact that he was being detained under the Mental Health Act 1983.

'Yes,' Sharief replied.

'How do you feel about the possibility of being here for a month or so?' I asked him.

'I'm fine with that because if I went back home it would be very dangerous for me,' he said. 'I would be targeted by very serious violent criminals.'

Sharief seemed like a lovely person and was clearly very bright, but at the particular moment, he just wasn't making much sense. After he was admitted as an inpatient, he spent two months in hospital being stabilised; when he was discharged, he was able to go home and went on to cope well with support in the community, which was really heartening to hear. I didn't see him again but I couldn't help wanting to know more about what he had been going through when I met him and so I decided to dig a bit deeper into psychosis.

Paranoid delusions of the type that Sharief was having are listed among the commonest symptoms of psychosis but some people experience the flip side of paranoia during a psychotic episode: they develop grandiose beliefs about themselves; they believe they've suddenly got elevated status (I remember one lady telling me once that she owned Concorde) or have been sent on a special mission. As psychosis can also be a symptom of bipolar disorder, which features extreme shifts in mood from low to high, I also wanted to hear from someone who had experienced it within this context. I met Paul through an online support group for people with bipolar disorder in Oxfordshire; he told me that he had experienced both types of delusions, paranoid and grandiose, really early on in his illness.

People usually develop bipolar disorder before they are 20; it sometimes develops later but rarely after the age of 40, according to the charity Rethink Mental Illness. When I spoke to Paul over Zoom in September 2021, he talked me through its onset, when he was 19. How does it start? I wondered. Are there any warning signs?

'It started like the source of a river,' he told me. 'It was just a trickle to begin with. As it gathered momentum, it became a stream and before I knew it, it was a river.'

The depressive (low) symptoms of bipolar disorder include lack of energy, low self-esteem, difficulty concentrating and suicidal thoughts; among the manic (high) symptoms are restlessness, agitation, elation, racing thoughts and impulsive behaviour. For Paul, it began with anxiety, perhaps made worse by the academic pressure of trying to get into a top university. He started to feel depressed and stopped sleeping; lack of sleep led to a heightened sense of anxiety and sensitivity, and deepened his depression. That's when psychosis first set in.

'I started thinking I was the cause of the world's problems,' he told me. 'I'd see someone on the news and think they were talking directly to me about stuff that I'd done. I remember there was a gas explosion in a block of flats that I thought I'd caused because I had been through the area a few days earlier.'

He felt very low and paranoid for the next three months but managed to work at a botanic gardens to earn money to go travelling. Did anyone close to him recognise that he wasn't well? I asked.

'People in the family could see that I was feeling low but my dad wouldn't accept that there was anything wrong with me. He'd say, "Don't be silly, take a caffeine pill to pep you up or have a whisky." He was dead against me seeking help because he couldn't accept that a son of his could have mental health issues.'

Paul went travelling for a few months and felt relatively happy again but when he came home, in the weeks leading up to starting university, he experienced an episode of mania and became convinced he could fly.

'It was the reverse of what I'd experienced before because this time everything was fantastic,' he said. 'I thought I could do anything. My only struggle was that I didn't really want to sleep because it seemed like a waste of time, and also that people couldn't quite keep up with my thought patterns. So the start of my bipolar showed up as two clear sides of the coin: a very long low followed by a very long high.'

Like depression and anxiety, bipolar disorder is thought to be caused by faulty neurotransmitters in the brain, including noradrenaline, dopamine and serotonin. These are the chemicals responsible for controlling the brain's functions. 'From the little we know, it's an imbalance of these chemicals that causes the problems,' Paul said.

There is also evidence of a link to genetics: family members of someone with bipolar disorder are slightly more likely to develop it, compared to the general population.

I was curious to know whether Paul experienced voices as well as delusions and, if so, what they sounded like?

'They seemed like loud thoughts that I was hearing internally as different voices,' he said. 'They weren't shouty loud but they were loud enough to sound like voices.'

To someone who hasn't experienced anything like it, hearing voices sounds like a scary experience. But Paul said that the voices themselves weren't a source of anxiety because, immersed in the psychosis, they seemed so real; it was more his thoughts and beliefs that affected how he felt.

'For instance, when I felt responsible for the fire in the flats, I was scared that the police would come and arrest me. But when I thought I could survive without sleep, I wasn't scared at all; I was invigorated.'

Did he ever actually try to fly?

'You have voices coming in from different directions, so there was probably still a small part of me telling me not to do something like that,' he says. 'I think there's always a bit of you that's lucid and knows you're going through an episode. That's my experience of it, anyway. I never jumped off a building or anything like that but it was a dangerous time because it was my first psychotic episode and I couldn't consciously identify what was happening.'

His stepmother took him to a psychiatrist and he was diagnosed as having hypomanic disorder, which was described to them as a milder version of bipolar disorder. I wondered how it felt to be told you have a potentially lifelong mental health condition when you're a teenager. Was it difficult to accept it and put his recovery first?

'It's not something you want to be associated with at that age, partly because of the stigma,' he admitted. 'And when you go to a hospital for an outpatient appointment and see lots of older people in the waiting room, you can't help thinking that you'd rather be going to the pub with your friends or off surfing in Cornwall. It's not a part of life you want to know about and so you're unwilling to come to terms with it.'

The psychiatrist prescribed lithium, a mood-stabilising drug, and after a few weeks of rest, Paul went to university as planned, perhaps unwisely.

'I wanted to put it behind me and get on with my life but I don't think I should have gone to university that year. I probably needed more treatment at the beginning in order to get better, not just the mental health equivalent of a sticking plaster. I wasn't stable, I felt weak and went around telling people at university that I was on antipsychotic medication, which wasn't a good idea. And when I had a mini blip, the medication had to be tweaked and it took longer to feel OK again, partly because I was living away from home.'

Still, he stayed relatively well after that for nearly two decades: he went on taking lithium, started working, settled down and had three children with his wife, Lisa. Then, in 2009, when Paul was in his thirties, he relapsed after a locum GP – who didn't research his medication properly – prescribed him steroids for a chest infection. The steroids reacted adversely to the lithium and he experienced his second major psychotic episode.

'I took the steroids and completely crashed,' he said. 'I was, again, incredibly high, but in a different way: I was very conflicted about life, by which I mean that everything had increased emotion, anger, stress and turmoil around it.'

I asked him if he would be happy to describe what he experienced after he reacted to the medicine.

'I was very ill,' he said. 'At one point, I started crawling around the floor. I think I was trying to hide after hearing the church bells ring in our village because I thought they were calling me to a shotgun wedding and I had to marry someone against my will. Unfortunately, my children witnessed that and it affected our relationship. That was the low point, for me. They treated me with kid gloves for some time afterwards and we're still not completely 100 per cent.'

Later that night, at two o'clock in the morning, he got out of bed, opened a window and shouted out accusations at the top of his voice, blaming people in the village for various fantastical things. The next day, his wife phoned an NHS crisis team in Bicester and arranged to take him to a psychiatric hospital to be assessed.

'By this point,' he said, 'I thought I was minor royalty, touring the wards of the hospital. After I was admitted, although I wasn't actually sectioned, they wouldn't let me leave. I tried to escape and another patient told me that I was standing in a corridor for hours, shouting. But my perception of it was that I was having tea at the cricket club.

'I also had some really frightening moments when I was in hospital: I remember thinking that my children were locked in a box in my room and I could hear them calling, "Daddy, Daddy, let me out!" That was torture.'

He describes the three weeks of hospitalisation that followed as, 'essentially, getting my brain back, which involved lots of sleeping and lots of drugs.'

When he came out of hospital, he was in debt, his mortgage was in arrears and his business was on its knees. 'Basically, I lost everything, apart from my family,' he said.

For the next six months, he worked at trying to rebuild his business from a shed in the garden of the house he rented. I asked what sort of follow up was available from the hospital and he told me that it was mainly group therapy in the community. 'Basically, your follow up treatment was outsourced to you,' he said.

Yet he did find group therapy useful. 'Even though you've got your mind back, you feel really low when you come out of hospital because you're facing the fallout of your breakdown. For me, that fallout was very significant because I had a family to support and felt I had let them down. I was acutely aware that if I hadn't fallen ill, our lives would be very different. Group therapy helps you to value yourself and your uniqueness. You do exercises that help you come to terms with your life: for instance, we chose 10 or 12 tracks that had been important to us over our lives, in a sort of personal version of *Desert Island Discs*, and it helped a lot with people's self-esteem. There was also practical advice about how to access debt respite and claim benefits.'

Although there's clearly a lot to be said for this kind of community support, Paul no longer attends his local group. 'The time comes when you don't necessarily want to hark back to your crisis all the time and you want to move forward and get on with your life,' he said. 'You can't regret the past. You have to move on. But you can only do that when you feel stable in yourself,' he added.

He says that the key to staying well is to audit himself, so he monitors his symptoms and experiences by text, email and internet on a weekly basis, using an interactive self-management tool called True Colours.

'Every week, I report on my moods – on whether I've been overactive or under-active in every aspect of my life, including whether I've eaten, exercised or had sex more or less than usual – and it gets recorded onto a chart. It helps you, as the patient, self-monitor. So if I was really high in energy and excitable, I would know to go easy and not take on too much. It might mean withdrawing slightly from society so that I'm less at risk of saying and doing awkward things that I would regret later. Or it might just mean avoiding the latest documentary on a high school massacre, which would give my brain the chance to go down a nasty route.'

At times like this, he'll draw, read or play music. 'The more you live with bipolar, the more you learn to self-regulate,' he said.

I wondered if he had ever been tempted not to take his medication – or if he understood why someone like Sharief at Springfield hospital might decide to refuse to take his – as it's an issue I've quite often come across in patients who experience psychosis.

'It's completely understandable because you can have incredible periods of lucidity during an episode,' he said. 'I remember having some amazing thoughts about infinity: What is space and time? What is nothing? What constitutes infinity? It's well known that people with this sort of condition, if they're artistic people, can have quite creative times – at least, in part – when they're experiencing psychosis. I find that if I'm going to compose something musically, the best compositions probably come then. The big worry is that if you are medicated to the extent that I am, which is actually quite a lot, then does that in some way stultify your creativity?

Does the medication prevent you from being how you really should be?'

I can imagine that it could be really difficult to stay on track if you thought your medication was somehow suppressing your true self.

'But if you don't take your medicine for a long time,' he said, 'the risk is that you will climb to the top of the building and you'll jump off, thinking that you can fly. Or you'll go onto a train track and stand there thinking that you've got the strength to stop the train.'

Although he hasn't had a psychotic episode for more than ten years, Paul feels it would be dangerous to consider himself recovered and so he'll go on taking his medication, even though it has unwanted side effects, which for him include a thyroid imbalance.

'I'd rather not take medication but it keeps me on track and I don't want to risk going off the rails again,' he said.

I was really grateful to Paul for talking to me and asked him whether there was anything about bipolar disorder that he'd like others to be mindful of. He replied that he finds it annoying when people make light of bipolar disorder by using it to describe someone who is merely moody. 'It's a very serious illness that can deal you a nasty blow. To be properly bipolar is no fun at all.'

*

Managing a psychotic illness can be an ongoing, sometimes lifelong, challenge, but psychosis can also affect people as a one-off episode that they never experience again. It can be triggered by stress, trauma, drugs, alcohol, a prescribed medication or a brain injury or illness. It is usually, but not always, a symptom of a mental health issue.

I was keen to hear from someone who had experienced psychosis as a one-off. I knew from speaking to mums who had experienced postpartum psychosis that the delusions and hallucinations can be of a similar kind to those experienced by people with psychotic illnesses, but was it the same with drug mania?

In the course of researching this chapter, I was fortunate to be given access to an online group of recovering addicts in East Anglia and a couple of the girls opened up to me about experiencing drug-induced psychosis.

Lou, who is 29, said she first tried drugs 'after my older sister taught me how to skin up', at the age of 15. Ten years later, she had moved through alcohol, weed, speed, spice, heroin, GBH and ecstasy, and had lost her job as a lab technician; by then, she was taking crack cocaine several times a week.

'One night in 2019, I seriously lost the plot when I was smoking crack alone at home in my flat,' she told me. 'I hadn't slept for days and suddenly thought I was locked in a B&B. It felt so real and I was so confused that I climbed out of the window into the street. Even though it only lasted a short time, for about 15 minutes, it was the scariest thing to think I was somewhere else rather than at home.

'Around the same time – or it might have been a few weeks later – there was a rat in my dad's garage and my mind seized on the idea that rats were trying to invade my flat. I put mirrors all around the rooms so that I could watch out for rats behind me. It was so intense. I stayed up all night terrified that I was being attacked and put scissors in my hair to stab the rats I thought were crawling on my head. After that, I watched out for rats every time I was alone at home smoking crack.'

As someone who cannot stand rats (I'm legit terrified and don't go down into my own basement for fear there'll be one down there!), I can't imagine how frightening/exhausting that must have been for her.

'I was heavy into my addiction and it's a nightmare being addicted to crack; it's very traumatic,' she said.

Lou went to rehab just before the March 2020 lockdown. When she came out three months later, I asked, was it hard to stay clean with all the social restrictions then in place?

'I kept myself busy,' she says. 'I went to recovery meetings online every day, sometimes twice a day. Then I got a job in a communications company, working from home, and although I sometimes felt lonely and missed meeting friends face to face, I didn't want to drink or take drugs, thank God; I hope I never will again. I get PTSD when I even see a picture of a rat.'

Lena, who took crack for 18 months and got clean in 2015, says it's been years since she experienced cravings for drugs. 'If you get clean properly, you're never going back to that,' she said. 'At least, I hope not,' she added.

Lena told me about what was happening before she went to a rehab centre in Ipswich. She described it as her lowest point.

'I was living with a dealer by then and taking so much crack that I didn't sleep for nights on end,' she said. 'Everybody knows that crack gives you paranoia but I smoked so much of it, all day and all night, that I was psychotic. I was convinced that there were police inside the washing machine, watching me and my dealer. I sometimes hid in the bathroom for 18 hours a day, avoiding the police in the washing machine. It was hell; I had to smoke heroin to calm myself down. It was the only thing that got me to sleep and then I'd crash for two days.'

Sleep is a factor in all the accounts of psychosis I've heard. If you don't sleep for days, it seems your brain struggles to cope.

Alisa, who is now 28, admitted to the group that she went back to smoking weed for a few weeks during the lockdown. 'There was nothing else to do. Life was boring and scary. You couldn't go out,' she said. 'But I started getting paranoid, so I had to give up. Fingers crossed I don't go there again.'

I told Alisa that I'd read a survey conducted by the campaigning drugs charity Release, which found that some drug use in the UK went up by a third or more during lockdown. (As it happens, surveys of alcohol consumption found a similar number of people drinking more over this period as well.) I wondered if Alisa thought that some drugs were more appealing than others during lockdown?

'I can see why more people were smoking weed,' she said. 'You're not going to take ecstasy at home in front of the telly but weed can be relaxing when you're on your own, unless you're smoking really strong skunk, when you'll probably land up hallucinating.'

It's true that drugs researchers are increasingly finding links between high-strength cannabis use and psychosis. So I wonder if there's a connection between the increase in smoking weed during the pandemic and NHS data since published, which reveals that first-time psychosis referrals in the UK soared by 75 per cent between April 2019 and April 2021. Analysis of the data by the charity Rethink Mental Illness shows that most of this increase occurred after the first lockdown.

Whether or not weed is a contributing factor to the figures, it's an alarming situation. NICE guidelines state that people experiencing psychosis for the first time should be assessed within two weeks. If cases continue to surge, the NHS will need a lot of extra resources to meet demand. Otherwise, people will be waiting way too long to access treatment, potentially risking lives.

We're only now realising what a toll the pandemic took on people's mental health. An international team of researchers published a report in October 2021 showing that globally there were estimated to be an extra 76 million cases of anxiety in 2020 than would have been expected if the pandemic hadn't happened, and 53 million more cases of major depressive disorder. In the UK, we were also experiencing a spike in people experiencing psychosis.

Dr Hughes, one of the lead psychiatrists at Springfield, said that it had put a lot of strain on the staff working there. 'I think we're really feeling exhausted now,' he said. 'I can't remember when I last had a day off. There was a time when it got a little bit quieter, in some ways, and then the floodgates opened and we've got loads of people coming in: a lot of people really suffering with the lockdown and being very isolated.'

It was difficult for everyone but I really felt for Bex at Orchid: her job managing a mental health ward was difficult and problematic at the best of times, then you throw a pandemic into the mix and see a rise in first-time psychosis – I can't imagine how surreal, difficult and frustrating it was.

'The initial feeling was fear,' Bex said. 'The way we nursed changed completely. I lived in a hotel at one point – couldn't wash my clothes, couldn't cook food – to isolate from my housemates so I could continue coming to work.

'With mental health,' she went on, 'you can have somebody who has delusions and real fears – for them – about the world ending. They think there's going to be mass deaths and that's exactly what happened. So we had to carefully balance what was psychosis and what was people's genuine fear.'

When we talk about the heroes of the NHS, we can often, quite rightly, think about the doctors and the nurses on the frontline in intensive care. But we mustn't forget that people like Bex and Jack had their work cut out dealing with the mental health impact of the pandemic – and will be picking up the pieces for years to come.

Just as patients' diagnosis suddenly became more complicated during lockdown, so did their recovery. 'Mental health relies on social support for recovery,' Bex explained. 'But people weren't able to see their families. Once you pulled social support away, it was a big, big disaster.'

I thought Bex was remarkable in her empathy and care for the patients at Orchid and asked what had drawn her to her job as a mental health nurse. It turned out that, like a lot of the staff working at Springfield, Bex had lived experience of mental health.

'When I was young, I experienced a parent with psychosis,' she told me, going on to explain that when your parent experiences something like that and you are a child, you also experience it. 'So when he thought the devil was outside, I also thought the devil was outside, and I remember that fear.'

Jack said that he too had become a mental health nurse because of lived experience. He explained that he'd had mental health problems since he was 15, which began with an eating disorder; later, he went through depression that led to a suicide attempt.

'I think it's harder for guys to speak out about mental health problems,' he told me. 'When guys present to mental health services, in general it means that they are in absolute crisis because in general men don't seek help. So when they're seeking help you know they are at rock bottom.'

Bex and Jack felt that the work they were doing could really help people – and it was clear from watching them work that it really did. There was so much compassion in the way they dealt with patients in crisis.

'Those few hours that you do your assessment and you hold that problem for them – or you hold the crisis, and that fear for them – that can do so much in terms of how well they cope,' Bex said.

'I've cried with people; I've cried for people and I've cried because of people,' she admitted. 'But at the end of the day, I wouldn't do anything else. This is who I am.'

10

Race and Mental Health

Ramone and Amarno

In 1999, after a public inquiry into the 1993 murder of teenager Stephen Lawrence and the corrupt police investigation that followed, the Macpherson Report found that the Metropolitan police was institutionally racist. We were assured steps had been taken to address unconscious bias and stereotypical profiling within police ranks but 21 years later, amid nationwide Black Lives Matters (BLM) protests following the filmed murder of George Floyd in the US in May 2020, a select committee of MPs were told by campaigners and activists that police racism is still a massive problem.

For many Black people in the UK, it's an issue that never went away. Official figures for England and Wales for 2019–20 show that Black people are nine times more likely to be stopped and searched by the police than white people and although it's argued that there are underlying reasons for these statistics, it's still no wonder that trust in the police and criminal justice remains an issue for British people of colour.

Perhaps it's no coincidence that an echoing pattern of racial disparity can be found within mental health services. These are two key areas where you would expect to feel protected and safe as a citizen of a country like ours but a 2018 independent review of the Mental Health Act commissioned by the UK government found that one of the problems within UK mental health services is, 'The rise of coercion and the continuing legacy of stigma, discrimination and racism in society.'

People of colour make up about 14 per cent of the population of England and Wales, and come from very diverse communities. Three per cent of the population are African Black and Caribbean Black British people. In the course of my research and after various different (very insightful) conversations, it became clear to me that young Black men in Britain are one of the groups who are especially up against it and so I wanted to explore some of the reasons why they might be struggling with mental health issues.

The charity Centre of Mental Health put me in touch with Ramone, 25, a Black Caribbean British man and their writer in residence, who co-authored *This Is Me: A handy guide for schools to help young black men thrive* with Androulla Harris.

Straight out, Ramone said, 'If we're talking specifically within the Black male community, we've been taught to dislike ourselves.'

It's a pretty shocking statement. Could it explain why, at age 11, young Black lads are no more likely to present with a diagnosable mental health condition than young white lads, and yet by the time they are young adults, they are more likely to be identified as being in mental health crisis?

'We've been taught that we're less than,' Ramone continued. 'We've been taught that we're only good for sports, creativity, fashion and entertainment, and if you don't contribute in these ways, then what are you here for? If you do contribute in these ways, the minute the game or the song or show is over, you're forgotten again. So there's a real fight for acceptance, for value and belonging, and it's a very subconscious thing, for the most part.'

I wondered when Ramone thought that fight for acceptance begins.

For many, he said, it starts the moment they go to primary school. If you've been raised in a home full of love, this may be the first time you hear negative things said to you, or about you, and the stark contrast between what you're experiencing at school and at home may make you feel you can't talk to your parents about it.

'You'll be a bit like, "Wow, what do I do with this?" You're going to hold onto it and either withdraw into yourself and start becoming timid, or fight back and start becoming angry,' Ramone told me.

There's a danger, he added, that if a child goes the other way and becomes disruptive in class, he'll be labelled as a bad child, forever in detention, always in isolation, without any redemptive means put in place for him.

'But he's not a bad kid: he's just had things happen to him that he doesn't understand how to process and no one's taking the time out to sit down with him and talk him through it. Fast forward to when he's 16: this anger has built up and he's now become a rebel in society. Then he gets apprehended and put in prison. Wrong is wrong, of course. If you thief a store, there needs to be punishment for that. But if someone had tried to understand earlier on what this kid was going through, the outcome might have been very different.'

In 1997–2014, students from Black Caribbean families were three to four times more likely to be permanently excluded from school than white students. Ramone and his co-author's book, *This Is Me*, cites studies that suggest the reasons for this could include low teacher expectations, discriminatory attitudes to behavioural issues and a lack of cultural understanding in schools. Peer pressure and ideas of masculinity among young Black males are also given as potential contributing factors. I remember Dr Sean at Springfield hospital saying how important the role of school is in showing children what they could achieve in life. So, are our schools failing young Black students?

Research shows that young Black people growing up in the UK are more likely to face difficulties at school than white people and that this is a risk factor for poor mental health. Other risk factors include: poverty, living in unsafe neighbourhoods or in inadequate accommodation, and the wear and tear of everyday racism.

This Is Me evolved out of an initiative by the Midlands-based Shifting the Dial, a partnership that brings together the Centre for Mental Health, the non-profit consultancy First Class Legacy, Birmingham Repertory Theatre (The Rep) and Birmingham and Solihull Mental Health NHS Trust to work to improve young Black men's resilience and wellbeing. In March 2019, they held an event to discuss how the needs of young Black men could be better met by the education system. Teachers, school staff and young Black men in Birmingham were invited along to talk about how to make school a better experience for them all.

Black representation on school staff and leadership teams was identified as being key to providing positive role models to Black students. Teachers were encouraged to be more aware of unconscious biases and how they could help improve the school environment for young Black men, bearing in mind their high rates of exclusion and low attainment. Several contributors agreed that both teachers and students need to focus on better communication and understanding.

One young person suggested: 'Instead of saying, "Sorry I'm late," say, "Thank you for waiting for me." As long as you give out a positive persona, people can bounce off of your energy and give you positive feedback. As young Black males, we need to break the stigma [and] the stereotypes.'

Another said: 'We need more teachers who get to the point – not, "Where's your tie?" but "Do you need a tie?" – immediately offering help and not embarrassment … if his [a student's] shirt isn't tucked in, he just needs to be taught that's not how he can move on in professional society … through this white-centric world in which he is so undermined and forgotten about and pushed under.'

This Is Me recounts how, at the event, 'One youth project lead shared an anecdote about his support of a child who had been excluded from school for having a "cultural haircut", and the distress this brought him and his family. The exclusion led the child to ask his parent, "Mum, why do I have to be black?" The project lead described him as "another young boy now lost in the system".'

One of the key recommendations made by this guide for schools is that teachers and staff need to recognise the cultural and psychological challenges a young Black man may face outside of school and strategically find ways to counteract that narrative, if it's negative, in approaching his education.

'As soon as we step out [of our homes] we have eyes on us 24/7, it has a huge effect on mental health … you constantly feel that you're being watched and judged,' one young man is quoted as saying.

'Teachers need to consider the underlying reasons for young men's behaviour,' the guide points out. 'For example, a young man in a single parent household may have additional duties and responsibilities (such as cooking, cleaning, contributing financially) and therefore may want to act "as a kid" at school.'

Ramone told me that, while he was at school, he didn't feel like he had anyone to help him understand what he was experiencing. He remembers being spat at by a so-called friend: 'I was really confused and thought, "Why did you do that?" The other kids with us didn't say anything and we just moved on as if nothing had happened.'

A 2020 report on racism in the UK commissioned by the YMCA found that 95 per cent of young Black people have heard and witnessed racist language at school. Ramone now looks back and suspects that his friend was expressing attitudes that he didn't necessarily believe but was under pressure from his parents to hold: 'It was almost like it wasn't about me. He spat out of disdain for what was going in his household and I was the recipient of it.'

A strong memory from primary school is the day some of the kids in Ramone's class instigated a fight between him and one of his friends. He and his friend were the only people of colour in their class. 'Half of them were stood around me and the other half were stood around him, really egging us on, saying, "He said this about you: you're not going to take that, are you?"

'They stirred things up until break time when we said, "OK, fine. Let's go fight." So, me and him had this fight and the rest of them were just watching and laughing – hysterically laughing.

'The fight got broken up; later that day, I was at my friend's house, because we were family friends, and we just moved on, like it didn't happen. But now I think about it, that was just entertainment for those guys to have us fight each other, which is really strange.'

Ramone says that he dealt with his confusion by withdrawing into himself.

'It's only now that I'm able to even face some of the things I've been carrying for however many years. It's really interesting because I wasn't very sporty or creative at the time, and I wasn't this amazing, popular fashion person, so I thought, "What am I here for? What is my use?" But when I met people from the Centre for Mental Health, they said, "Actually, writing is good – people need that as well." I was like, really? Huh? Shout out to those guys – they spoke some life into me and said, "This is actually valuable to the world." I was like, OK, sure! So I'm kind of running with it now.

'Just to think that if I'd just had that sit-down at primary school, if I'd had someone to help me process these things that were happening and say, "OK, this is what's going on ..."' Ramone said, breaking off wistfully.

It's gutting to think it was more than ten years before he found value in his abilities – value that a teacher could have helped him start accessing at primary school. He was good at English and creative writing but feels that, one way or another, he was discouraged from growing his talent. Instead, he was presented with a template. 'I was told, "This is where people like you fit in and these are your options."'

In *Against the Odds*, a short film available on the Centre for Mental Health website, narrator Alex says, 'It's psychologically damaging to think, at that young age, that you're different, that you can't do anything and that your life is almost over before it begins. When you're almost mentally segregated and pushed away, it's going to cause immense mental problems.'

Ramone thinks that it would help if children were taught about their identity as early in life as possible. 'When you go to school, there are so many ideas put before you: be this, be that, do this, do that. If you do this you're a good boy, or will be popular; if you do that you're a bad boy, or will be unpopular. If you do this you get five value points, if you do that you lose three value points – it's a fight for value. Nobody will consciously say this but this is what I perceive to be going on, especially in the transitions from child to adolescent to adult.

During these transitions, so much is being suggested to you about what your value is.'

I wondered what racism meant to him.

'In my thinking, racism is someone saying, "I do not like you because your skin colour is different from mine,"' he said. 'So, what does that mean? Are we talking about heritage? Do you not like me because we have different heritage, or bloodlines? From what I can see, people have mixed and migrated throughout history, so when someone says to me, "I don't like Black people," how do they know that, tracing their line back far enough, they won't find a mix? I don't think any of us can say we're pure bred – so you don't like me because our ancestry is different but if you look back far enough, what you don't like is in you.

'Racism is just an understanding of identity. So we should learn about identity, what makes up a human being, what that means and why it's important. So, then, if I'm not creative, I still have value. If I don't have this particular shade of skin tone or I'm not part of that social group, I still have value. Rather than saying, "You can achieve anything," to kids, I think it's better to say, "There are so many boxes – and your unique, individual fit is important."'

It wasn't until his final year at college in 2012 that Ramone started thinking more about the impact of race and identity on his life. 'Until then, I was in a bubble, I just cared about partying and games. They were the pillars of my existence. The news didn't exist; the pressure didn't exist. Nothing else mattered.'

The bubble burst when he started hanging out with an old friend who had recently come out of prison to find his support network had vanished and a complete lack of state aftercare. His friend had an extremely jaded view of society that both informed and upset Ramone as they grew closer.

I totally get that because when I was very young I used to go about with a boy who went inside – and when he came out, although he looked the same, his way of thinking was radically different. It was like he walked out as another person entirely. And there's often no support for people when they come out of prison. A lot of lip service is paid to rehabilitation and reintegration but sometimes all they get is a train ticket.

'I developed a learnt hopelessness,' Ramone told me as he recalled his friend's influence. 'I started drinking a lot because I felt hopeless and didn't know why and I couldn't admit how I was feeling, because I thought it was a sign of weakness.'

There's a massive stigma around mental health within the Black community, he said, but he overcame his reservations to go to counselling, which was helpful up to a point. 'I definitely received a level of healing through it but it didn't take me all the way. It highlighted the roots of my lack of value but didn't give me an effective way to deal with it. So now I was drinking because I knew why I felt bad and didn't know what to do about it.'

In 1965, the first UK Race Relations Act banned racial discrimination in public places and made promoting racial hatred a crime. Further Acts expanded the legislation to outlaw other forms of discrimination, including racial abuse. These days, you could argue overt racism isn't anywhere near as visible as it was in the 1950s and early 1960s, when it was legal for landlords to advertise vacancies with the caveat: 'No Irish, no blacks, no dogs,' and racist trolls on social media face jail. But in a subtler form it is still being experienced on a daily basis by people of colour.

Some of my friends have told me about experiencing what are known as micro aggressions – which are everyday comments or actions that subtly, and maybe unconsciously or unintentionally, communicate a negative or stereotyped attitude towards them. Micro aggressions can seem like barely anything: a woman clutching her bag or blatantly putting her phone away when walking past you; a shop assistant following you around a shop or ignoring you in favour of a white person at the till; being told by a white person, 'I don't see you as Black' or asked, 'Where are you from?' and lots of other examples. Some people criticise the term 'micro aggression' for underplaying how belittling the behaviours can be; others feel it sums up how subtle but hurtful they are.

Sometimes, Ramone told me, he'll sit down at the end of a day, 'and I'll think, "Wow, that happened?" It was so subtle and quick that I didn't notice it at the time.'

Psychological studies have shown that daily hassles can build up to be a bigger source of stress than huge events like a bereavement or trauma. Daily hassles are described in these studies as the irritating, frustrating and distressing demands that people face on a day-to-day basis: arguments, disappointments, rising prices, being put on hold, losing things, being late, worries about appearance, crime. If too many of these daily hassles build up, people are more likely to get depressed and anxious, or have a mental health crisis.

Ramone began to experience social anxiety; he felt nervous going out and thought everybody was laughing at him. Each new small failure or rejection added to the pressure and he found himself using destructive behaviour 'to escape the reality of these things that were happening to me,' he says. As his depression deepened, he binged alcohol, smoking, sex, food and games, though all of these made him feel worse. His romantic life was toxic and his drinking became so heavy that he thinks he was in the early stages of alcoholism. Then he crashed his car. A romance broke up. He reached breaking point.

Feeling overwhelmed, he stockpiled bottles of wine and sugary snacks and necked alcohol and sweets in his room for an entire week.

'I look back and wonder how I got through it all and wasn't hospitalised,' he said. 'It scares me now to think about it.'

Finally, he felt so desperate that he cried out to God for help, 'and that began the process of being free from these things that are not evil in themselves but become a problem when you over-indulge them.'

Luckily, he had some pals around him who said, 'Come on, you're letting yourself go. Let's do something about it.'

His mates took him to church, which started the redemptive process that he'd longed for, although he understands that it's not going to be the answer for everyone.

It can be enlightening, he said, simply to focus on your own individual existence in nature, to reflect on how incredible it is that just one sperm – out of all the millions of sperms – fertilised the one egg that created a unique embryo that grew into an individual person – that's you. And that you had no control over any of it – no one does – so whether accidental or miraculous, it is extraordinary.

'So, don't worry about your value because you have innate value, just by being here,' he said.

He's so bloody right about that!

I asked him whether he thought that social media had helped to open up the conversation about mental health. 'The rise of technology has helped in some ways,' he said. 'I've found comfort in blogs and forums where people can come and to and fro. But social media doesn't help in other ways because you've still got the Twitter trolls.'

It's a blessing and a curse, I agreed. (Although, increasingly, Twitter is feeling like such a trash pit, tbh.)

'I have a love/hate relationship with Instagram,' he added.

It's funny, isn't it? We're both adults and understand that we're seeing curated images on social media that don't reflect reality but you still find yourself comparing your life to the one you're being shown.

'I've been given the notion that better things exist,' Ramone said. 'I then step out to get the better things and when it doesn't work, I sulk for a bit and then try again. That's been my cycle for the last five years. Still, things have got better. I'm not where I want to be but I'm not where I was, so I try to be content with the process. I'm on my path, on my journey, at my pace.'

I asked him where he would put himself mentally now.

He said he still struggles with confidence and self-esteem issues. 'Sometimes, I have to say, "You're a liar!" to that voice in my head that puts me down. Because I do matter.'

He's determined to break the cycle and move forward and is modest about his achievements so far. 'Hopefully, there will be people who benefit from the work I produce,' he said.

Clearly his work with the Centre for Mental Health – the *This Is Me* guide and blogs and other contributions – are already doing their bit to raise awareness and help change attitudes.

'My passion is the overall wellbeing of humanity rather than specifically within a particular race,' he added. 'It may sound naive but can we all just get along?'

I mean, wouldn't it be great?

Ramone's experiences feel familiar to those of another Black Caribbean British man I met through the Centre for Mental Heath. Amarno, aged 25, is a student and a talented visual artist; he's also a peer researcher at the centre, helping to gather stories from people in underserved communities most affected by mental health difficulties.

I asked Amarno if he had a first memory of being judged for the colour of his skin and if he'd be happy to share it with me.

'This is hard for me,' he said, 'and I think it's safe to say that a lot of my peers would feel the same: we've experienced racism all our lives but we never really took it as that. It was more a case of, Oh, it's just the teacher, or, Oh, it's just this person just being mixed up.'

Despite being a bright kid, Amarno felt that he was considered a troublemaker at school, partly because he asked a lot of questions in class and partly because of his appearance. He recalled some of his white teachers having a problem with it when he was made a prefect – he overheard them saying, 'How did he get the prefect role with that Afro, and the way he behaves and dresses?'

'I felt I couldn't achieve excellence in my own space and be myself without somebody having an issue with it,' he said. 'But I didn't really understand why.'

There's a sense, he said, that Black men are held to 'a different account emotionally' to some of their peers. Media representation of white men show them as having a full range of emotions but you don't see the same range in Black male representation, which reinforces stereotypes.

He told a story of how he was present when a white teacher at his school refused to let a Black student leave the classroom and when the student made for the door, she accused him of pushing her.

'She had blocked the way and he said, "Can I get out, please?"' Amarno recalled.

'No, you're not going anywhere!' the teacher said.

'He grabbed for the door and she started with the dramatics, saying "He hit me! He hit me!"

'Later, the head of year came to me and two other guys and asked, "Did it happen?"

'"Sir, I don't even like this guy," I said (because me and him had had a feud for the previous two years). "But I'll tell you now, he never touched her."'

'There is an underlying sense that just our mere presence alone is a threat,' Amarno explained. 'We are seen as the predator or the aggressor straight away, especially around white women, and so there's this idea that Black people, especially Black men who operate in a white space, have to keep self-censoring to make white people feel comfortable.'

He doesn't bear the brunt of overt types of racism because he is light skinned, he said. This is due to light-skin privilege and colourism, which is a form of racism that discriminates between people on the basis of their skin tone.

A few days before I spoke to Amarno, I'd been making a film about a child model in a Black family whose mother was an American model and father was Nigerian. The mother told me that colourism was huge for Black girls in modelling. The darker girls were always being told, 'You're not quite right. It's not quite what we were after.' And then the girls with lighter skin would get the bookings, but they would still be 'seen as Black girls' – and the casting directors could say, 'We've got a Black girl.'

'Black girls experience that a lot,' Amarno agreed, 'and it's the same on the Black male side but in reverse, so the darker you are, the more masculine you appear to be, versus when you are light skinned you are perceived to be more feminine, more emotional, more erratic, more romantic … the word that they use on the internet now is "simpin". Which is basically like you worship a woman or something. You will bend over backwards to please a woman.'

Yet, despite his skin tone, Amarno still experiences racism just because he's young, Black and male, he said. And when he experiences it, he often feels he has to moderate his reaction. 'That can play out in the workplace as well; I've experienced situations where I've had to self-censor and hold in my frustration for fear of how it would be viewed, especially with managers.'

He added that he has issues 'facing both ways' because of 'the anxiety of living around Black males in general, in a city'. He spoke about this at a Black forum recently. 'I gave an example of how, when I'm walking towards another Black guy, who's around my age group – and I think this is uniquely faced by 16 to 25 year-olds – our bodies will tense up, almost as if we're ready to draw, like cowboys in a Western. It's that internalising of danger experienced from our peers but also living in a system like Britain that adds to the pressure. What's funny is that the last time it happened, as I got close to the guy, I realised that he was somebody I knew from primary school and hadn't caught up with for years.'

When he left school, Amarno decided not to go to university and instead tried various jobs and volunteering but couldn't find any bigger purpose in what he was doing. At work, he sometimes experienced discrimination that he found confusing.

'I used to have locs,' he recalled, 'and even just having locs was hard because the first thing people would say to me was, "I love your locs! Do you smoke lots of weed?" I'm not in that experience but I still have a version of Blackness imposed on me.

'One day at work, one of my sub managers came up to me and said, "I don't like the soap you're using in your hair. The perfume is too strong." It was only Head and Shoulders so I don't know what he was on about, but some of my colleagues were Black and they said, "Yo, he's being proper racist. How come he's never said that to anybody else?"

'I was the only person there with locs but there were girls with long hair who used fragrant shampoos and he'd walked past them without saying anything. Still, I didn't know if it was racism or if he just didn't like the shampoo, and I'm someone who is slow to anger, so before I took it further, I asked around, "Does my hair smell?"

'A Polish girl working there said, "I use Head and Shoulders. What's he on about?"

'So I took it to another manager, who was Asian, and explained what had happened. "It's probably nothing," he said. He seemed to think it wasn't worth talking about.

'I went to another manager, who was white, and he said, "He's probably just playing with you," and dismissed it.'

Not being believed when you call out a racist action or behaviour is sometimes known as racial gaslighting – when people say things like, 'Oh, I'm sure he wasn't being racist,' 'You're probably being oversensitive,' or, 'Maybe he was just in a bad mood.' Daily stresses like this and a sense of lack of purpose sent Amarno's self-esteem plummeting and he became anxious but felt he couldn't share what he was going through with his friends. He said that it's common for young Black males to feel isolated in this way.

'In our friendship groups, we may share on a surface level but we don't really go deep into our feelings because we haven't been socialised to express these emotions or to unpack them. So, even when I was trying to speak, I still couldn't articulate how I was actually feeling.'

He became depressed: 'It was a combination of daily hassles becoming a life stress and also an existential crisis,' he explained. 'I was thinking, "Why am I here? What am I living in this country for? What is my purpose?" I never had a clear understanding of who I wanted to be or what I wanted to do and the pressure of succeeding in a place like England made me spiral into a lot of negativity, thinking, "I'm not going to achieve stuff; I have nothing to offer." So it led to a lot of anxiety about what I was going to do in my future. It got to a point where I was really low and didn't want to get out of bed; for days on end, I only got up when I had to go to work.'

I wondered if he recognised that he was depressed.

'I thought it was just me and that I was just being an idiot and a loser. At the same time, I could see that my body didn't want to do anything – everything I was interested in when I was younger, I didn't want to do anymore. I didn't want to go outside; I was always in my bed.'

I asked how low he got during this time?

'I grew up Christian and had internalised the idea that if you take your own life, you go to hell, which was a saving grace in a sense because it meant that there was no way out. You either had to implode in life or just give up in life but you could never kill yourself. Still, the body will find other ways to try and get rid of you: I stopped eating, started sleeping a lot, didn't want to do anything. There was lethargy and lack of emotion that I thought was just laziness.'

His girlfriend at that time gave him support and encouragement but nothing seemed to help.

'Then, one day, I got drunk off my head and was mad listening to music and drew exactly how I felt about my frustration and anger in an A4 booklet. When I woke up the next day, hungover, and saw what I'd drawn, I thought, "Yo, that's how I was really feeling!" I had found a way to articulate what I was going through. I felt so much peace at that moment and thought, "I need to do this again, but minus the alcohol."'

Using art to express difficult feelings led Amarno to create a body of work about his journey through mental health called 'Katharsis', which he exhibited at a Birmingham gallery in early 2020, just before the first lockdown. The work was partly inspired by his involvement with the Red Earth Collective, an arts, drama and music company that specialises in mental health, and a Black forum run by First Class Legacy that put him in contact with other young men like himself. He called it Katharsis, which means 'purging emotions, particularly through art,' he said.

At his exhibition, people were drawn to Amarno's self-portrait with a cage around his head, a representation, he explained, of the hell you can create by being trapped in a cycle of negative thoughts and emotions.

'That image resonated with a lot of people,' he said. 'They had experienced the same emotions that I had but they had never considered them from a visual perspective.'

Another piece that attracted attention was 'Rage', a self-portrait with wolves circling his head.

'The title refers to the rage that has been bottled up for years,' he explained. 'It's anger that has not been addressed because of a societal and cultural pressure to suppress emotions, a pressure which is even more acutely felt by those who are Black and male living in England and dealing with racism, implicit bias and unconscious bias, whatever that is.

'I internalised my anger because I felt pressure as a man to hold in my emotion. The raging hounds surrounding me in this image represent how individuals feel an angry aura around them while simultaneously reaching boiling point. For me, this has also led to physical symptoms like muscle tension and stress headaches. So that's the kind of thing that Black males experience in different ways when we walk around in society.'

It's a challenge having to repress yourself as a Black person and as a male, he added.

It's an incredibly obvious thing to say but clearly I have no idea of what it's like to be Black and how draining it must be to experience micro aggressions day after day. Like Ramone, Amarno thinks that the build-up of pressure can be so great that many young men react by either imploding (for instance, through drug and alcohol abuse) or exploding (gang violence, crime and domestic abuse). Partly because his father and grandfather are role models in their communities, Amarno felt that neither option was possible for him. 'But I knew that I had to get these emotions out of me, so I used art to expose them but also to validate them and exorcise them.'

He had tried talking therapy but felt he was being 'handled' and told what he was feeling, rather than being listened to or heard, by someone who didn't understand his cultural background.

He studied CBT online and found it more effective than counselling. 'Now I know to say, "Stop! Feel what you're feeling. Don't make any assumptions. Reframe it later."'

Words can fall short when articulating certain emotions and pressures, he told me. 'What I've experienced when dealing with Black people, or people of colour, is that we can know what we're talking about without actually saying anything. So, oftentimes, when I've been around my friendship group of Black males, our sentences will end with, "... you get me?' or '... you hear what I'm saying?' and we will have expressed something that we all understand without actually having to say what we're saying. I don't know if there's something spiritual about it but I would say it's a vibrational energy, where we are in tune from an ethnic perspective. Hopefully that doesn't sound convoluted. I don't know how to articulate it into words and I think this is an issue that is facing Black people living in the West: some things we cannot explain through words and articulate in a manner that is middle class and correctly punctuated; some things are just felt. That's why it was big for me to use art to articulate my feelings, especially being a part of Red Earth, who work with the Black Caribbean community using the arts to explore these types of issues.'

His consciousness grew as he attended lectures by Kehinde Andrews, professor of Black studies in the School of Social Sciences at Birmingham City University, Akala and other experts in this area who shed light on the experiences of British Black people. 'It was a revelation,' he recalled. 'I realised, so *this* is what has been going on and happening to me.'

Amarno is now a student at Birmingham University studying International Relations and Development and he works as a peer researcher at the Centre for Mental Health, where one of his roles is to interpret what is being said in the gaps left by the young people in peer group meetings and surveys.

'Often I am able to codify that into middle-class language and explain what it actually means, as well as capture the emotion in the room at the time.'

Meanwhile, he finds himself confronted by implicit bias at uni, he said – the mental judgements and associations that people unconsciously make because of social conditioning, even if they are anti-racist.

'When I enter a space, it's like, OK, shall I be the so-called Black person that they're expecting?' he said. 'Or, if I'm just myself, will they think I'm trying to be white? There are a lot of things you have to walk through in your mind, especially if you understand sociological theories about race and ethnicity. It can be taxing but if I allow those thoughts to overwhelm me, as they did before, it means I'm not in control: I end up being imposed on and can't move forward and have agency. The whole point of Katharsis was trying to move towards gaining that agency and understanding that you are a sovereign being, you control your environment as much as you can. What happens to you is how you interpret it and you just have to step wisely in that space.'

That makes absolute sense to me.

I have nothing but respect for Amarno and Ramone and for their courage and steadfastness in navigating a world that evidently looks very different to them than it does to me. I'm grateful to them for being kind (and patient!) enough to give up their time to explain their experiences to me. This book is about opening up the conversation about mental health and they have helped me to understand more about what young Black men are up against. Their clear-sighted analysis gives me hope that change will happen the more we become aware of what is actually going on.

11

Poverty and Mental Health

Jenny, Sam and Nicola

So where are we now? At the time of writing this final chapter, the future still seems very uncertain: the world is coping with the fallout from the Covid-19 pandemic and the collective trauma of the last couple of years. It has been a really, really difficult time for everyone.

In an ideal world, medical science will prevail over the virus but its onslaught and persistent presence continue to trouble us, physically and mentally. No one is unscathed – and our mental health services and the amazing people working within them have been among the worst hit. Like the staff on hospital ICUs and other wards and services throughout the NHS, they've never been busier. They need and deserve our support more than ever.

While we were filming *Back on the Psych Ward*, I met and reconnected with many remarkable members of NHS staff who didn't hesitate to turn up to work during the early days of apprehension about how Covid-19 would evolve. While almost everybody else remained in relative safety at home, as key workers, they continued to help people throughout the pandemic, despite (I'm sure) feeling sometimes vulnerable and scared themselves. I found their courage and resilience just so inspiring. And selfless.

At times, people admitted that they were exhausted and I often heard members of staff saying, 'I can't remember when I last had a day off.' But they chose to come in to work because their skills and compassion were so desperately needed.

And some of them had to adapt in really innovative ways. Springfield hospital houses the National Deaf Services and staff on the deaf wards wore special issue see-through face masks so that patients with profound hearing loss were able to see their mouths for lip reading. As if the whole PPE mandate wasn't enough to deal with! But every member of staff I spoke to expressed their willingness to do anything they could to keep themselves and their patients safe.

With one eye on the news every day, we saw some harrowing reports on how the pandemic was affecting people in different parts of the country. Things were bad everywhere but they were much, much worse in areas where poverty is more widespread: England's poorest people were almost twice as likely to die of coronavirus than the rest of the population, which must have added untold anxiety to an already frightening situation. And these were also the places where a mental health crisis was already unfolding, pre-pandemic.

In 2019, analysis of GP surgeries across England by the House of Commons library showed that in some of the poorest pockets of England – which are mostly in the Midlands and north east – nearly a quarter of people were seeking help for depression, around seven times more than in some of the richer areas. The worst off, Brinnington in Stockport, Greater Manchester, had an estimated neighbourhood prevalence of depression at 23 per cent, whereas in one of England's richest areas, Townshend & Zoo, Westminster, London, it was 3.1 per cent.

According to a report by the Mental Health Foundation, 'The likelihood of our developing a mental health problem is influenced by our biological makeup, and by the circumstances in which we are born, grow, live and age. Those who face the greatest disadvantages in life also face the greatest risks to their mental health. This unequal distribution of risk to our mental health is what we call mental health inequalities.'

Unemployment, poor physical health, social disadvantage and daily stresses are known to be some of the biggest risk factors for mental health disorders. Pandemic containment measures came after ten years of austerity and massive cuts to council budgets; during lockdown, families with children at home found themselves having to spend more on food, heating and childcare, and food banks recorded a sharp increase in uptake of emergency food parcels, especially those going to children. The UK government increased Universal Credit by £20 per week to cover extra lockdown expenses, but the rise was only temporary and ended in October 2021.

'I met a mum whose kettle had broken and it put her in a real dilemma – do I buy a new kettle or buy food?' said Father Alex of St Matthew's Church in Burnley, Lancashire, one of the most deprived local authority districts in England.

Father Alex and Pastor Mick of the charity Church on the Street Ministries were featured in a harrowing BBC News report about their work to feed and clothe the poor in Burnley during the pandemic. The report brought many viewers to tears, went viral and attracted £250,000 in donations from the public, which was desperately needed. 'I lost count of the number phone calls I had from ladies in middle England saying they just couldn't believe what they had seen on the news,' said Father Alex. '"Is this *really* happening in our country?" they asked me.'

I too vividly remember watching the segment, feeling floored by the idea that so many people were struggling and suffering. Their pain was so evident.

Of course, Burnley's problems haven't gone away now that lockdown is behind us, he said. There has been record demand for mental health services in East Lancashire; several media outlets have reported that services are overstretched (and not just in Burnley but throughout the country). Father

Alex runs a breakfast club and a food bank out of St Matthew's Church. He says that some of the conversations he's had with breakfast club users have been very revealing about mental health in his community.

'One chap came up to me and said, "Can I have a word?" and we went up to the altar and he said, "Father Alex, I'm fucking drowning and I don't know how to stop myself from drowning."'

Although the man was in debt, his main problem was alcohol but he had been told he couldn't access rehab until he had been 'dry' for two weeks. 'I can't stay dry for 20 minutes,' he told Father Alex despairingly. 'I can't get out of bed without a can of cider, so to stay dry for two weeks is impossible.'

This particular individual understandably felt let down that the help he was being offered was so conditional. 'Some of the people who come to us have lost their trust and faith in the social service provider,' Father Alex explained, 'so I think we've become a bit of a safe haven where they can come and unload and just tell it as it is. The sadness for me is that I don't have the expertise to make them all well. I can offer them prayer, which I hold great value to, and signpost them to professional services; then they drift out the door. It's a very transient community, so you see them come and go and quite often you're left wondering how they are and where they are. Are they being provided for? Or are they sleeping in a car park somewhere?'

He hears a lot of upsetting stories from homeless people. He recalls meeting a young man who had left university during lockdown, had nowhere to go and was placed in temporary accommodation for the homeless in Burnley. 'But he couldn't bear being in that environment; the chaos and noise were a constant torment,' he said.

'I also met a couple living in a tent on the canal, who lived there by choice because to them it was better than the hostel, which they said was too violent and too threatening. That says something to me about what we do with our young people who aren't on a pathway to success. When you hear talk about people "falling through the gaps" these are the people I think about. What a sad indictment of our social services and our care providers that these people would rather live on the canal in a two-man tent, with no toilet facilities or place to cook! They asked me if I could provide them with food that doesn't need heating up and there's me giving them a couple of carrier bags of biscuits. It's just horrific; it's deeply distressing.'

Until recently, young homeless people were often sent away to a hostel in Blackburn, he says. 'That was horrendous for young kids of 18 and 19. They had already been separated from their loved ones for numerous reasons and were then told to get on a bus to a place they didn't know where they would spend the next 48 hours,' he said, adding that it still happens now but is more of a last resort than it used to be.

'I don't want to make this about politics but I listened to Boris Johnson's election address the other day and thought, "Sounds wonderful, this levelling up agenda. Why is it that people in the Ribble Valley get more than people who live 25 miles away on the far coast in Blackpool?"' he said, referring to regional health and economic inequalities that were debated in Parliament in October 2021.

There's a lot that needs to change, he thinks. 'You'd like a world, wouldn't you, where somebody says, "I'm struggling with my mental health; I've got nowhere to live," and there's a place in our society, which is one of the richest countries in the world, where we say, "OK, we'll house you and we will provide you with immediate care for your mental wellbeing"?'

'But the reality is, we'll send you to another town and we'll put you on a waiting list that could be four weeks minimum and could be up to three months. For a young person who's in crisis, it's an absolute travesty. It's a disgrace, such a dreadful indictment of our society.'

Part of the problem, he thinks, is that people don't care about each other enough. It's what you'd expect a vicar to say, perhaps – but maybe less so the story he uses to illustrate his point. While he was having a few days in Blackpool with his family in 2020, he was approached by a guy asking for a couple of quid. As he handed over some change, a passerby said to the guy, 'Get back in the fucking sea, you dirty piece of shit.'

'Did he just say that?' Father Alex's teenage daughter asked.

'What does that say about our general care for people in these situations?' Father Alex asked. 'Even in my own church, when I started the breakfast club and brought in the food bank, I had questions like, "What's in it for us?" and heard people say: "Why are we doing this? It's not our job." These are people who've been Christians for a lot longer than I have.

'Well, I think you'll find it is our job,' he said. 'That's what our primary calling should be, but sometimes it feels as if in many ways, we've forgotten how to look after and care for people.'

Father Alex is 52 and has lived in Burnley all his life; he has never known the town to be free of areas of deprivation. 'Poverty is a pandemic in itself and it has never been dealt with. Nobody has ever solved the problem. That's not a statement against any particular government; it's a statement against our society.'

The mental health impact of poverty is all too clear to see. 'Even people whose mental wellbeing is strong are feeling the struggles of Covid,' he said. 'I feel knackered. Every day is tricky, a bit of a trek, but I'm very fortunate: I've got a lovely house and a lovely family; I've got a few quid in the bank. But a lot of people don't have that: they live in rented accommodation; they're getting by on a shoestring budget. It's not unreasonable to expect them to care for their children and educate them but these people can't cope; it's too much for them.'

There are several social housing estates near St Matthew's but it's the private rentals where tenants are suffering the most, in the vicar's experience. 'I know of circumstances where young people have said, "It's just horrendous – I've got a flea infestation; I've got rats." They approach the landlord and the landlord says, "Well, I'll come and sort it but I'll need to put your rent up for doing it." Those kinds of things happen all the time.'

A 2021 study by Shelter suggested that people in approximately 1.9 million households could be suffering physical and mental problems as a result of poor housing conditions, struggling to pay the rent and living with the constant threat of eviction. Rents are rising nationwide as demand for properties outstrips supply.

'Some people's housing conditions are just horrific,' Father Alex says. 'I remember a Hungarian mum who came to see us. She was living in the worst house you could possibly imagine, on a street where there was drug dealing and music being played through the night. I've never seen somebody so desperate for help and because we had attracted some media attention, we could make a difference and she was rehoused. That was one of the good news stories – sometimes it's a case of literally frogmarching people to the front desk and saying it's not acceptable.'

He says that having to resort to using a food bank is a trauma in itself for some people. 'We've had mums come in physically shaking and trembling with fear because they're feeling ashamed that they need to come and get a food parcel. There are people who come to us who are working and the cost of living just got too much for them, and it's very difficult for them to come in and admit that to you. They feel a lot of humiliation about asking, "Can I have a couple of toilet rolls? Could I have a box of cereal, or a jar of coffee?" A family jar of coffee is four or five quid and that's a big impact. In fact, I think that some of our guys would just prefer three or four jars of coffee because some of the food is affordable but coffee, cereal, bread and milk become a daily expense.'

He worries that the picture he paints of Burnley is very grim – 'but it's a wonderful place,' he said. 'It's absolutely beautiful. We're in a valley, surrounded by beautiful countryside. Where I live, very close to the council estates, there are some woods that have wild deer living in them; it's a fantastic place to go for a walk.

'There is a lot of work in Burnley as well,' he added. 'It's not a place that's on its arse in terms of job vacancies. But many people aren't equipped to work. You've got to give them the skills to think about what they can offer: What can they do? What do they like to do? Ask some of these people to write a CV and they wouldn't be able to do it. And it's a lot to ask them to talk about themselves in a positive way when their mental health has been so badly affected by their circumstances and the addition of Covid.

'So you say, "Well, look, you can do this, or you might be good with your hands, or good creatively," or whatever it is that will give them a platform to sell themselves to employers.'

He adds that there are a lot of single parents in Burnley who are faced with a salary-versus-benefit scenario: 'Is it worth my while going to work if I only earn £10 or £15 more for working a 38-hour week than I would being at home?'

What about Burnley's schools? I wondered. Are they overstretched like mental health services?

'I think an awful lot of credit needs to go to our schools,' Father Alex said. 'They are a complete lifeline for a lot of people; they are filling the gaps. They are the foundations – the bricks and mortar – for many children. But as one head teacher said to me, "We're only there from nine till three o'clock and then we hand the children back to the parents and carers. We're not there in half term; we're not there in the summer holidays."'

St Matthew's is affiliated to a church school and two secular schools. 'The teachers I've seen in action are completely inspirational,' Father Alex said. 'I don't know how they do it, especially as there's often one or two unruly kids who are just trying to disrupt everything. So the teachers are my heroes through the pandemic because they've just kept going, working in the evenings and through their holidays in an attempt to keep the kids on track. But it is a two-way thing and parents have got to take that on,' he said. 'They have got to be able to take it on.'

Father Alex knows several mums who belong to a Monday support group called Women for Peace that meets in the community centre near his church, and who mostly live on an assisted housing estate nearby. I was interested in finding out about their experiences with mental health services in their area, and where they thought investment was most needed and would be best utilised. I was really pleased when they agreed to contribute to this chapter.

'I've done six weeks of therapy on the NHS and I found the group a lot better,' said Sam, a softly spoken mum in her thirties, who has made three suicide attempts. 'I started going to the group because of my anxiety and depression,' said Nicola, 50. 'My daughter was already going and she said, "Come along with me," and I tagged along. I found it really good: it helps me out; I can relate to the people there. We can get our troubles off our chest and know that it will stay there in that room. It won't go any further.'

'We always say, "What happens in the group stays in the group,"' added Jenny, a chirpy mum of five who travels from another area of town to be at the group every week, 'so you can air your stuff and get it out and we don't go sharing it. There are about 15 ladies when we all turn up and honestly, we talk about all sorts of different things. A lot of the ladies have got mental health problems – there's a lot of anxiety

– and I think it just gets everyone together. Some have two or three kids but there are ladies there with a lot of kids and they talk about the turmoil they're going through. We're all going through similar situations, so even though it's a wide range of people, everyone knows where you're coming from.'

Three of Jenny's five children have autism and one is non-verbal. When it comes to mental health services, she said, 'I think you've got to fight to get any help. It's a constant battle. You've got to ask for everything. There's a lot of mental health problems in Burnley, just from our point of view,' she continued. 'There's been a petition to put up fences at Gannow Top bridge over the motorway because there's all these people wanting to kill themselves and there's no places to help them.'

'Our area is really in need of more resources for depression and mental health,' said Nicola. 'We are really under-resourced.'

'Everything's just a struggle to get hold of,' Jenny said. 'I've got a daughter with mental health issues – she's 14 and during lockdown she was self-harming and trying to kill herself. She's ASD and probably bipolar as well; she's very up and down. She took her first overdose in July and we didn't even see anybody until February, and that was on Zoom, so it was seven months before anybody even looked at her. And that's just one case.'

I was really shocked to hear this. If a teenage girl's life was in danger because she'd had a physical fall or accident, the nearest hospital would send an ambulance to try and save her. Why aren't the same resources in place to rescue that same teenage girl from her life-threatening mental state?

In July 2021, the NHS set out proposals for new mental health access standards, including a pledge that patients requiring urgent care will be seen within 24 hours of referral, if not sooner, if their need is very urgent. These proposals are very welcome and will save lives, if they can be implemented, but how are people who are suffering mentally going to cope in the meantime?

'They say, "If she does it again, ring the crisis team,"' Jenny said. 'And so the second time she did it, I rang the crisis team. "Well, is she doing it now?" they asked.

'I said, "No, it was earlier today."

'"Then it's not a crisis. Ring your doctor."

'So you go and see your doctor, who says: "You've got to wait to see the paediatrician." And you wait six months to see the paediatrician on a Zoom call.'

I was keen to hear from Jenny what help looked like when it finally came.

'Everyone we've seen says, "Oh, it's just her autism." Well, it can't just be her autism. I don't know many autistic people trying to kill themselves and thrashing around and the like.

'My daughter says she has a constant feeling of hopelessness and wants to kill herself four or five times a day but they signed her off their books because she hasn't hurt herself in about a month. They say, "She's recognised it – and because she's autistic, it's probably because she's had a really bad day or she doesn't like the subject she's doing in a lesson." They say, "She can't rationalise it."

'"She *can* rationalise it," I say, "because she does it." But they just fob you off. And then she'll try to kill herself again or self-harm, or whatever.'

Sam nodded in agreement. 'I've tried to take my life – I've taken a couple of overdoses,' she said, 'and when you go for help, they just fob you off and send you to different places. "Ring these numbers if you need help." You wake up in the hospital and then they give you a piece of paper with numbers to ring.'

Sam belongs to a church community and found support among her friends there: they came to the hospital with her after one of her overdoses, sat up with her all night and helped her home at 5am the following day. They stepped in because the care she needed alongside life-saving medical intervention was beyond the hospital's resources. Sam recognises that without her church community, her recovery would have been that much harder.

At home, Sam is her grandmother's carer and her son is experiencing suicidal feelings, a situation that Nicola can very well relate to. Nicola had her grandson living with her until recently. 'His mum couldn't have him living with her anymore,' she said. 'It was too much for her and the other three children living with her. He's threatening to kill himself, so we've sent him to the mental health unit at Blackburn hospital, where he's been seen for ADHD and other issues.

'Now, I've just come out of hospital because I've had operations on my legs for deep vein thrombosis but I'm expected to work, so I've had to send him to his dad's because he was just too much for me. I'm trying to get on the disability – I've been waiting about eight months to hear – but no luck, as yet.'

The difficulties of living with a child in mental distress cannot be overestimated, these mums agreed.

'They don't hurt themselves with what you'd think, like a razor blade or compass,' Jenny said. 'My daughter opens cans of pop with can openers and harms herself with that; she harms herself with random stuff – things I would never have thought about being a danger, until all of this. Anything she can harm herself with, she will harm herself with. She smashes glass all the time and even if you vac it up in her bedroom, there are always shards of it left on the floor.

'It got worse during Covid, because she wasn't seeing her friends and there were no services available, with everyone being in lockdown. That was probably half the battle but it's still bad – there's still nothing out there to help her. It's terrible.'

Jenny and her husband feel they were unfairly held responsible for their daughter's actions.

'When my daughter took her first overdose, me and him got the blame. They said, "You shouldn't have had tablets in the house,"' she said. 'But you don't know your kids are going to do that – otherwise I wouldn't have had them in the bloody house. They were only paracetamol but we got told off because we had them. So we threw everything out – we don't have owt anywhere now – and then she's done it again and they said, "We told you to lock up the tablets."

'I said, "We don't have any tablets in the house but they're 18p at Aldi and when she's all dolled up, she looks old enough to buy a packet of paracetamol. I didn't even know she had them."'

I wondered if Jenny had an idea of what sort of help might benefit her daughter.

'I can't fault the schools,' she said. 'The funding is a lot better and they seem to have a lot more resources and support in place than in the past. My daughter's on a suicide watch scheme because she's self-harmed, and they've got electronic registers now, so if she goes out of the classroom for a wee or whatever, she's got about five minutes before they come and get her.

'I don't think therapy would be any good for her because she'll just tell them what they want to hear. Kids shut off when they're with officials who talk to them in a medical manner.

The doctor says, "Is everything all right?" and your kid says, "Yeah, everything's all right." He says, "That's good. You've done this course, and you've done that, haven't you?" She says, "Yes," and he signs her off.

'But she's just started helping out on a youth stall and she seems to like that, maybe because it's more about being in a social group. You've got to be referred to the group, to make sure there's no bullying and whatnot, and there are council workers there who are all properly trained. They talk to the kids, not in a medical manner, but more in a general manner, so I think they get a bit more out of them.'

'What about yourself?' Father Alex asked.

'I don't know. I don't think about myself,' Jenny replied, breaking down into tears. 'I don't go anywhere. I just do groups, me.'

'The non-medical interventions seem to work better than the medical, from my point of view,' she said, when she felt better. 'You get your ten minutes with a doctor and they're not really listening to what you say but you go to the group, let it all out and you feel better after it. So I think the groups are a better option, although people do obviously need the medical bit as well.'

'The communities are the main key,' Nicola agreed. 'If we had more investment in the community, it would be better than putting it into doctors and nurses because it's up to the community to start the ball rolling.'

'You need things on the ground to start off with, really,' Sam said. 'The group is good at nipping a problem in the bud before it grows. It's like a little family.'

'Everybody thinks about everybody else and it takes your mind off thinking about yourself,' Jenny added.

'And if you've got something that somebody else might need or want, you think, "I'll pass that on,"' Nicola said.

'It could be something-and-nothing,' said Jenny, 'but it's nice to think you're helping someone.'

It seemed from what they were saying that they thought community and social networks were needed as much as the mental health services, if not more so. And for their kids, who were the main source of their worry (along with paying their heating bills over the winter), they felt there wasn't enough going on outside school for them.

'They need social clubs because there's nowt to do,' said Sam.

'There's Scouts and Guides, which are great, but everything else just costs so much and when you've got five kids, you can't afford it,' said Jenny. 'Free clubs would help to set up community networks and the kids would learn discipline and other social stuff there. My kids don't listen to me but they'll listen to somebody else. Clubs would give them structure and authority figures but they're too expensive. My daughter likes her group, so maybe more outreach schemes are a good idea.'

There's real wisdom in what these ladies are saying: it's the communities that count; it's social networks that make a difference; it's coming together that helps us get stronger. If loneliness and isolation are bad for our mental and physical health – as bad as smoking 15 cigarettes a day, some reports say – then social connection can be one of the antidotes to poor mental wellbeing. It's what people have been saying forever: you get by with a little help from your friends.

'The council used to fund the community centre where our group meets but now they've pulled back and said, "Oh, you can fund it yourself,"' Jenny said. 'But obviously, we need thousands for the centre. A lot of other groups meet there – they do a luncheon club; we have something for the older ladies, a teenage group, a nursery and kids' groups. Everyone's trying to raise money to keep it all going – there are Christmas sales and crafts fairs and tombolas, and it's all volunteering. It's a constant battle for all the groups to raise enough to pay the council tax on the building.'

Every group member pays a weekly contribution; one way or another, they find the money to keep it going, even though, as Sam said, 'What you get on benefits is only just enough to feed the kids.'

I wondered if any of them struggled to put food on the table.

'I'm all right with food,' Jenny said, returning to her chirpy self. 'Bills are more of a worry than food. Trust me, I'd never go hungry. I'd start eating my family before I went hungry; I'd go through Aldi's bins. We live on pasta because you can make big pans of that – every night I cook up a big cauldron. The amount of stuff I make with pasta is unreal. When you've only got about £20 to feed everyone, pasta is the best dish.

'But just some help with gas and electric would be nice because that is going sky high. I pay monthly for mine and start worrying about my next instalment the moment I pay it. Everyone's worried about something, aren't they? And then the kids leave the lights on.

'At the moment, I'm struggling for a pram for my youngest, who is autistic and non-verbal. He's too big for a normal pram, so the paediatrician has put in for a disability buggy because he puts his feet down now and it overtops the pram. I'm having to beg everywhere to send me a pram and I've been waiting for months now. There's no rush their end. I rang up and said, "Where the bloody hell is this pram?" and they said, "'Oh, they've shut the factory down in England. It's in Spain now and we're waiting for the manufacturers." There's no end in it. I still haven't got a date when I'll be getting it.

'You think to yourself, "Stop waiting and just bloody buy one yourself," you know. But not everyone's that lucky, are they?'

I've never claimed to be an expert on mental health; this book was always about opening and encouraging the conversation and giving those directly affected a platform to take control of the narrative. In the course of my research, I spoke to experts and looked into a lot of different studies and surveys, but the most important lessons I learnt came through listening to people's stories and hearing their points of view.

So, I'm incredibly grateful to everyone who has shared their feelings and experiences with me – in the hope that, in doing so, they could help others. A massive thank you to all the people involved for their help and guidance, and also for their honesty and trust. This book wouldn't exist without them.

Useful Resources

Samaritans

Samaritans aims to provide emotional support to anyone in emotional distress, struggling to cope, or at risk of suicide.

Website: samaritans.org • Helpline: 116 123

Email: jo@samaritans.org

You could also go to your local A&E, contact NHS111 or make an urgent appointment to see a GP or your psychiatrist or care team.

Rethink Mental Illness

Rethink improves lives through its network of local groups and services for people who are severely affected by mental illness, including an advice service, online resources, carers services and advocacy. A wealth of accessible information about mental health is available on its website.

Website: rethink.org

Mind

Mind is a campaigning mental health charity and a fantastic online source of information and advice for people with mental health issues, including where to get help, treatment options and advocacy services.

Website: mind.org.uk • Helpline: 0300 123 3393
Email: info@mind.org.uk

Beat

Beat offer information and support to people of all ages, no matter where they are in their journey.
You can access a one-to-one web chat on their website or ring their helpline:
Website: beateatingdisorders.org.uk
Helplines: 0808 801 0677 (England)
0808 801 0432 (Scotland)
0808 801 0433 (Wales)
0808 801 0434 (Northern Ireland)

Refuge Against Domestic Violence

Refuge offer a range of services for supporting women, children and men who have experienced violence and abuse.
Website: refuge.org.uk
National Domestic Abuse helpline: 0808 2000 247
You can also visit www.nationaldahelpline.org.uk to access live chat (Mon–Fri 3–10pm)

BeGambleAware

BeGambleAware offers free, confidential help and support to anyone who is worried about their – or someone else's – gambling.

Website: begambleaware.org (offers a live chat advice service)
National Gambling Helpline: 0808 8020 133
The NHS also offers a directory of addiction services:
Website: nhs.uk
NHS Northern Gambling Service helpline: 0300 300 1490

Stonewall

Stonewall is a human rights charity that stands for LGBTQ+ people everywhere and campaigns for LGBTQ+ rights, equality, education and awareness.
Website: stonewall.org.uk

MindOut

MindOut offers an Online Support Service (including Instant Chat) which is available globally, as well as mental health services for LGBTQ people aged 18+ who are based in Brighton and Hove.
Website: mindout.org.uk

The Consortium of Lesbian, Gay, Bisexual and Transgender Voluntary and Community Organisations

The Consortium has a searchable directory of services aiming to strengthen and support LGBT+ groups, organisations and projects.
Website: consortium.lgbt/member-directory

The Proud Trust

Find an LGBTQ+ youth group near you through The Proud Trust. They also offer links to trans specific, young people of colour LGBTQ+, digital and schools youth groups.
Website: theproudtrust.org

2BU Somerset

Groups, information, outreach and support for LGBTQ+ young people in Somerset.
Website: 2bu-somerset.co.uk

OCD-UK

OCD-UK is a national, recovery-focused charity run by and for people with obsessive compulsive disorder; its website is full of information and links to a network of support groups.
Website: ocduk.org

YoungMinds: Fighting for Young People's Mental Health

Online support and resources for young people with mental health problems and a free textline for young people experiencing a mental health crisis, including psychosis.
Website: youngminds.org.uk
Childline: 0800 11 11
Textline: Text YM to 85258

PANDAS: PND Awareness and Support

PANDAS offer support for people struggling with pre or post-natal depression. They have a free helpline, but also provide email support, social media and Facebook groups and information on their website.

Website: pandasfoundation.org.uk

Helpline: 0808 1961 776

APP

Action on Postpartum Psychosis offers a peer support service for women and families affected by postpartum psychosis, along with information, training, awareness raising and research. You can also email them to request one-to-one peer support.

Website: app-network.org

Email: app@app-network.org

Centre for Mental Health

Centre for Mental Health is an independent, not for profit thinktank dedicated to eradicating mental health inequalities and fighting injustice by changing policy and practice.

Website: centreformentalhealth.org.uk

Black Minds Matter

Black Minds Matter offers resources and therapists relevant to Black individuals and their families.

Website: blackmindsmatteruk.com

Acknowledgements

Thanks to Gordon Wise, Jacquie Drewe, Yvonne Jacob and her team at BBC Books, Dr Sean Whyte and everyone at Springfield University Hospital, my *On the Psych Ward* film crew, Rebecca Cripps and all the mental health charities and contributors who made this book possible.

Index

Index

Index